Pack It Up

TRAVELING SMART & SAFE IN TODAY'S WORLD

To Sarah + Shane —
Happy Travels!

Anne

Special thanks to the travelers I have met around the globe who have contributed many of these invaluable travel tips.

Copyright © 2004, 2003, 1996, 1990 by Anne McAlpin
Illustrations Copyright © 2004, 2003
The Ultimate Traveler's Checklist © 2004, 2003

Cover and text design by Garred Design, Inc.
Illustrations by Holly Herick Design
Back Cover Photo by Christopher Briscoe

ISBN 0-9627263-1-1
Library of Congress Number 90-082758
Printed in the U.S.A.
10 9 8 7 6 5 4 3

Published by Flying Cloud Publishing
For more information, contact:
www.packitup.com

To my father whose sea stories enticed me to travel to the four corners of the world — to experience my own, and my mother, who continually packed my suitcases to ensure that I made it in one piece.

This book is dedicated to my parents, both of whom have made the ultimate journey.

TABLE OF CONTENTS

Appendix:
Resources /To The Traveler/Notes & Quotes

"If you want to get away from it all,
don't take it all with you."

Anne McAlpin

-1-
Before You Go

"If you want to get away from it all, don't take it all with you". This always gets a big laugh at our Pack It Up seminars. Most people know they pack too much when they travel, but aren't really sure how they can bring anything less. How do you travel safely, pack everything you need and travel lightly? After reading this book, you'll be on your way.

This book is a compilation of over 25 years of travel tips that I've discovered on the road. Some I've learned the hard way, many I've learned from more experienced travelers I've met along the way. There are even a few tips that I learned while studying in Europe and realized too late that I didn't have the budget or the strength to carry everything I thought I needed!

You'll find valuable plane tips I've picked up from other frequent flyers (whom I'm always interviewing in the air) and cruise tips that I learned while working aboard cruise ships. Check out the Family Travel chapter for invaluable tips on traveling with children and find out how to save money on laundry services in Laundry on the Go.

One of the biggest concerns of women traveling alone is security. I've addressed this important topic in the security chapter, which also includes tips on how to prepare your home before you leave, and what to pack in your security wallet.

You'll find invaluable luggage tips, packing tips and yes, even tips on how to get through airport security more efficiently with plastic bags.

And...no need to take notes about all the great items you'll want to remember to pack, everything is listed at the end of the book in, **The Ultimate Traveler's Checklist.**

These are the secret travel tips that I've discovered from traveling to over 65 countries that will make any trip safer and a whole lot more fun. And remember that "travel" happens the minute you step outside your front door. Whether you're flying to Europe, taking a cruise of a lifetime or driving to a family reunion. You still have to pack to get there. So, let's get started.

**Three important steps to a successful trip:
Read, Ask & Plan.**

READ anything you can get your hands on about your destination, from the travel section in the Sunday newspaper to the internet to guidebooks. Before you rush out and spend money budgeted for your trip on travel books, check out the library to find out which guides fit your needs specifically. If you don't have access to a computer, most libraries provide them and they have a wealth of information on any destination in the world.

ASK family, friends, and travel agents questions about your destination. People love to share their experiences and their knowledge. How often have we all received invaluable information through a casual conversation? Your reading should prompt many questions and now is the time to find the answers.

PLAN ahead. Advanced planning can save you money and help alleviate stress further down the road. By planning and asking, you may receive many discounts that you were unaware existed, from pre booking savings to off-season and senior discounts.

Tips

■ There is nothing more valuable than a good travel agent. Many people do not realize the amount of time and money travel agencies can save them. Keep in mind there is usually a fee involved for airline tickets, etc. however, time is money, and for many this fee is worth the time they would spend searching for the least expensive airfares on their own. Call and compare prices for all your travel needs.

■ Surf the internet. Many great travel bargains have been found on the internet. However, be sure you understand any restrictions that might apply to any purchases. And, as mentioned above, there's nothing like working with a reputable travel agent to protect you and your travel plans. The majority of travelers still prefer to use the internet for research rather than making purchases.

■ Learn how to read an airline ticket if you don't know how. It's all too common for travelers to be left stranded, because they didn't know how to double check the departure date or time on their ticket.

■ Just like brands of food, different travel agencies have different features and benefits.

■ If you have time, call the toll free numbers for the airlines listed in your phone book and see what, if any, special flights they may have available.

■ Check all your travel documents! Make sure the airline listed on your ticket jacket is the same one you will be flying on. This is a problem many travelers run into after they are dropped off at the airline terminal.

■ Always reconfirm your domestic airline ticket 24 hours in advance and your international ticket 72 hours in advance.

■ Obtain or renew your passport for International travel. The normal processing time to obtain a passport is six weeks, but it can take longer during peak travel months. Locate the passport facility nearest you at the State Department's website www.state.gov

- If your travels require visas (another good reason for using a travel agent) you should apply for your passport at least six months in advance to allow time to acquire them.

- Have a full medical and dental check-up.

- Obtain or renew your International Driving Permit.

- Review your travel, homeowners, automobile, and medical insurance policies to determine coverage for trip cancellation, interruption, loss, theft, accident, or injury while traveling overseas. If necessary, consider additional coverage.

- Research to find out if special precautions (such as inoculations, malaria pills, etc.) are required for your destination.

- Check with your pet sitters, plant sitters, and child care. Have a second choice on standby just in case someone has to cancel at the last minute.

- Obtain a calling card from your long distance telephone company before leaving home (or buy a pre-paid phone card). This will expedite any calls you must make and put an end to searching for correct coins in foreign currency.

- Be sure that your bills are paid and up to date if you plan to be gone for an extended period of time. Better yet, pre-pay in advance & you won't come home to a stack of over due bills.

- Photocopy the pages in your travel guide for your own use so you don't have to take the entire book along. Or simply tear out the applicable chapters.

- Check the expiration dates on your credit cards, passport, driver's license, medical certificates, camera film, vitamins, medications, etc.

- Notify your credit card companies that you'll be traveling & using your cards at your destination.

- Put your name and business address in your coat. They are always being left in restaurants, planes, and trains.

■ Use blank index cards (or recipe cards) to record special events on, such as birthdays and anniversaries that will occur while you're away.

■ Bring along special occasion cards & you're ready to go. This saves last minute shopping (and money) in strange cities. Of course, you might like the charm of greetings cards in another language. They make a nice souvenir.

■ Pack even lighter & just carry a few "generic" cards than can be used for any occasion. I travel with cards with pictures from my home region.

■ Purchase some sticky address labels and spend an evening addressing them to all your family and friends (or print the addresses right off your computer). When you are traveling, no need to haul your address book with you. Just peel and stick. It's easier and faster and you will know who did and didn't receive postcards!

■ Bring self-address labels for your own use — for safety, you may want to use a Post Office Box label. Use them as return address labels on mailing, for filling out forms in stores or checking into hotels. Makes life easier when you are tired.

Research Your Destination

■ Check the video store for videos about your destination or ask your travel agent. They don't have to be travel guides specifically. For example, you may see feature or fictional films about France that include local customs, history, and scenery.

■ Look into educational tours related to your profession. They could be tax-deductible and save you money.

■ Call, write or email the Chamber of Commerce or National Tourist Office for additional information on your destination. Ask specifically for maps, dates of events, or whatever you are interested in. Addresses can be obtained at local libraries or the telephone book.

■ Research tour companies. Specialized tours, such as sports tours, art tours, etc. are a great way to meet people with the same interests and sometimes save money.

■ Minimize culture shock by learning about the lifestyle & foods of your destination.

■ Familiarize yourself with local customs and political differences to avoid offensive behavior, inappropriate dress and breaking the law.

■ Borrow some language learning tapes from your local library. Learn a few key phrases before you need them. If you're really serious about learning a foreign language, check college extension courses, or buy tapes and take them and a small cassette recorder with you.

-2-
Security at Home & En Route

The most important safety tip is to be aware of your surroundings. In this day and age, any city can be dangerous, even your own home town, no matter what size or population. The idea is not to travel in fear but to pay attention to some important details with which you can protect yourself, your home, and your property — and not only while you are on vacation. Many of these following suggestions apply to everyday circumstances. Most of them are common sense.

General Home Security

Before you leave:

❑ Put timers on several of the lights in your house, and for a good deterrent, leave your radio tuned to a talk show.

❑ Obtain an engraving pen from your local library or police station and mark your valuable electronic equipment with an I.D. number.

❑ In cold climate zones, turn off your hot water heater and defrost the refrigerator in case of a power failure. If you live in temperate climates, turn down your furnace and air conditioning.

❑ Unplug your appliances such as your computer, stereo, and television in case of power surges.

❑ Affix screws into window frames to secure them from outside opening. Ask at your hardware store for additional ideas.

❏ For added security to sliding glass doors, place a broom handle in the track. Also, a board across the center of the window placed on two rivets will do the same trick.

❏ Lock all your valuables in a safe deposit box.

While a weekend outing may require no arrangements for your home, a longer trip requires some consideration. Don't advertise that you're away by having your newspapers pile up in your driveway or allowing your lawn to grow wild.

❏ Have your mail held at the post office for your return.

❏ Have your newspaper stopped or have a reliable neighbor pick it up everyday.

❏ Don't forget to also stop UPS delivery or any other service that usually frequents your home.

❏ Hire a gardener to take care of your garden and keep your lawn mowed.

❏ If you don't have an answering machine, put your telephone on the lowest ring setting so that no one outside can hear the continual ringing.

The following are other things you can ask a neighbor or relative to do while you are away to help give the appearance that you are home:

❏ Place their garbage in yours once in awhile.

❏ Shovel snow from your sidewalk and/or driveway.

❏ Park their car in your driveway after 5pm in the evening and on the weekends once in awhile.

❏ Check your mailbox periodically for any mail or advertising that might have slipped through.

❏ Keep a set of your car keys in case there is a fire in your garage, or any other reason your cars need to be moved.

❏ Check the inside of your home periodically in case there has been any kind of water damage, frozen pipes, or anything that they might be able to assist with until you return home.

❏ If you have an answering machine, ask a friend to check it and answer any messages that sound important. Calls unreturned for any length of time are a good give-away that you are not at home.

❏ Leave contact information & insurance numbers with a neighbor just in case.

Security En Route

■ Be sure to always travel with a security wallet. Please see page 26 for more information.

■ A card with typed telephone numbers and names of relatives, bank account, insurance company, etc., can be very helpful in case of an emergency. Don't forget to include a neighbor in case you just can't remember if you remembered to turn off the iron! Keep one copy with you at all times, and pack another in your luggage.

■ Separate from your wallet, carry a list of the items in your wallet, including the phone numbers to call to report the items lost or stolen.

■ When traveling alone, always use valet parking when available. Walking through a deserted parking lot alone is not a good idea anywhere. Be sure to give your car only to a uniformed valet.

■ NEVER carry anything for anyone for any reason.

■ Keep your distance from stray luggage and packages left
   unattended in airports and other public places.

■ Never leave your luggage unattended.

Hotel Tips

■ Always guarantee your hotel room reservation to a major credit
   card, just in case you are delayed on your flight or arriving
   transportation. When you are traveling alone, be sure to always
   have reservations.

■ When checking into a hotel, never give your home address,
   as it's a sign to burglars that you are not at home. Instead, give
   your work address (or Post Office box #).

■ Most hotels no longer print the room numbers on the keys, but
   in the event that they do, be sure not to leave your key in any
   position where strangers could see your room number. This could
   lead to problems later on.

■ If available, request a room near the elevator, to avoid the
   chance of someone following you and walking long distances in
   empty hallways.

■ Verify the exit route from your room upon arrival at your hotel.

■ Don't leave a "Please Make Up My Room" sign on the door,
   which advertises an empty room.

■ Avoid staying in a room in remote parts of the hotel or next
   to exit stairways.

■ To prevent extra hotel telephone charges and taxes, use a
   telephone calling card or cell phone.

■ In a hotel room or aboard ship, memorize the location of the
   nearest emergency exit. Count the number of doors in case of
   heavy smoke. Also, this works on planes in case the lights go
   out, you should count the number of rows to the nearest exit.

■ When traveling with children, be sure they know the name & address of the hotel. Put a business card of the hotel in their pocket.

■ Don't leave any valuables in your room when you leave. Experienced thieves know how to find what they're looking for. Place them in the hotel safe.

■ Ask the front desk which streets & neighborhoods to avoid.

■ Take some small 'post-it' notes to use on your hotel mirror as reminders. "Remember your travel alarm," "passport in the hotel safe," and so on.

Hotel Comfort Items

Whether you're on the road for two days or two weeks, it's nice to have some comfort items with you. Here are some "comforting" ideas:

Battery Operated Travel Alarm Clock

Don't rely on a hotel wake up call when you have to be at the train station at 6am. Have a back-up plan even if your hotel room does provide an alarm clock, you might not set it correctly. Bring extra batteries and put fresh batteries in your clock before the trip. Upgrade your old travel alarm clock to a new one that stays illuminated all night long.

Night Light

Take a nightlight for unfamiliar hotel rooms or ship cabins. It lights the bathroom just enough for a guide, if you are disoriented in the middle of the night. Leave a note in your bag to remind to pack it when you leave the hotel. Bring a converter if necessary.

Queen/King Size Top Bed Sheet

Ever wonder when the last time the bed spread was washed in your hotel room? Here's my secret. Upon check-in, I request an extra sheet and after I take off the bedspread I put the sheet on top of the blanket to protect me from a scratchy (and maybe not so clean) blanket. Leave a note on the bed in the morning to please leave the bed as is so housekeeping won't put the bedspread back on top of your clean sheet. Or you can travel with a light weight silk sheet. This way you know it's clean and it gives you bit of luxury away from home.

Fitted Bed Sheet
Don't you just hate it when you go to a hotel and sleep on the bed and the bottom sheet moves all over the bed? Consider taking your own fitted bottom bed sheet (shrinks down to almost nothing in a compression bag).

Collapsible Water Bottle
Save space & travel with a water bottle that folds up when empty. Here's a tip: I can' t get to sleep with cold feet so I take two: One for drinking water & one I fill up with hot tap water as a foot warmer.

Travel Toilet Paper
On my travels in Europe I often stay at "European-style" small hotels — clean, comfortable, but not always stocked with items I like, such as toilet paper. A small roll of toilet paper can be flattened, taking up very little space and adding little weight to your bag.

Washcloths
Don't forget a wash cloth, an item sometimes not found in smaller, non-luxury hotels.

More Hotel Tips

- Always have a stash of one dollar bills for vending machines, tips, and to put on the pillow each morning to tip the maid.

- Remember that if you did forget something most hotels have items available at the front desk (either complimentary or for sale).

- Most hotels have hairdryers in the room or you can borrow one from the front desk. Call ahead & confirm & you're packing lighter.

- Place your shoes in a clean pillowcase so your clothes don't get dirty and you can use the same pillowcase to sleep on during your stay if you encounter a scratchy hotel pillowcase. They also come in handy for dirty clothes.

- Hairspray makes for a quick room freshener in a pinch.

- Ever wonder what to do with the complimentary shower caps in your hotel room? In hotels where your room seems to be two blocks away from the ice machine, toss a couple shower caps in your bag when you leave for the day, then on your way back to the room, use it as an 'ice bucket' of sorts.

- Another use for a hotel shower cap is to bring it home and use it in the kitchen to cover large, odd shaped bowls.

- Sometimes the water at a hotel/motel is heavily chlorinated. Using the melted ice from the ice machine often creates a more pleasing drink of water.

- Concierges at major hotels are an invaluable source of information.

- Packing cubes are perfect for hotels because who wants to put their personal items (like clean underwear) in a drawer when you don't know what was in it before you checked in? A cube will also keep everything together (like a drawer within a drawer) so nothing slides to the back & gets left behind.

- Create a mini-spa in your hotel room — or at home! Just collect travel sizes and samples of bath gel, hair conditioning treatments, foot scrubs — whatever you've been meaning to try. They're especially great when traveling on vacation because being "stuck" in the hotel room means you have minimal distractions; great after a long day of traveling.

Tips for Women Traveling Solo

There is an old proverb that says, "It is better to travel alone than with a bad companion." I've traveled alone and with a bad companion I whole heartedly agree, solo is much better! For years women have asked me, "Aren't you scared to travel alone?" I'm happy to say that I've never encountered a really dangerous situation, because I try very hard not to put myself into one. Admittedly there have been some times when I've felt uncomfortable, like an unfortunate incident in a movie theater in Spain; however, things can happen just as easily at home as they can on the road.

I've traveled on my own for over 25 years and have only once been robbed. Guess where? Yes, in my own country in broad daylight. What I realized was that when I travel I always make sure to be aware of my surroundings, but when I was in a rush shopping downtown USA, I wasn't paying attention and my wallet was taken right out of my unzipped purse.

In addition to the afore mentioned security tips, here are some more tips for women traveling solo.

- If the desk clerk announces your room number loudly, ask for a different one. Strangers may be within hearing and harass you later. Fortunately, hotels are aware of this and henceforth are very cautious.

- Use the "peep-hole" in your door to see who is there before opening it. If you are the least bit uncomfortable, call the front desk immediately.

- When traveling alone, treat yourself to a nice bouquet of flowers to brighten up your hotel room. Use the ice bucket for a vase.

- Always leave the light on in your hotel room and the "Do Not Disturb" sign on the door (after the maid has cleaned) when you leave, to eliminate any unwanted visitors. And leave your TV turned on. While you are inside your hotel room, always keep the door locked (if it isn't automatically) and the chain across the lock (if provided).

■ To make you feel more at ease when dining alone, take a book or magazine to the table. Keep in mind that paperback books are hard to read if your meal requires two hands to eat it.

■ For safety it's a good idea to travel with a whistle. This can alert those around you that you need some assistance. My favorite is a whistle that is a combination compass & magnifying glass. I use the magnifying glass to read the tiny print in brochures and the compass is great for navigating a new city in a rental car. Clip it on your bag so it's always handy in the event you need the compass to find your direction when reading a map. Solves the problem of knowing which way is North when you exit a museum.

■ If you have an uneasy feeling about a hotel, don't hang the "Make Up My Room" on your door. Instead, locate the maid and advise that you'd like your room cleaned and that the "Do Not Disturb" sign be hung on the door when finished. Any steps that you can take to help secure yourself and your surroundings are worth the extra bit of time and effort.

■ Travel with an inexpensive door wedge for added protection in unfamiliar surroundings.

■ If you are a single woman traveler and find yourself in the situation of a foreign man harassing you, sit beside a local woman on the train or bus, or walk directly behind women. Even though there often is a language barrier, women tend to stick together and can understand your look of distress towards an overly friendly male pursuer.

■ Sit in the front of the transportation or restaurant you are in. Take precautions that you may not necessarily always take at home: Don't walk through parks alone if you feel the least bit nervous in the situation, and don't walk outside in the evening without a companion. Don't unwillingly put yourself in a position in which you might be endangered.

■ Always travel with a flashlight so you won't be caught in the dark. I prefer a small trael size flashlight that clips onto my daybag so I'm never without one.

■ Carry 2 plastic coated S-hooks (found in hardware stores) in your purse or carry-on. Use them in the hinge area in the bathroom stalls to hold your tote/purse/coat to keep them off the floor when there are no hooks available.

■ Another option to a security belt is to travel in travel skirts and pants from travel stores and catalogs that feature zippered "security" pockets. They are large enough to hold money and a passport and the bulk is easily hidden within the folds of the skirt.

-3-
Packing Smart for
Airport Security

We travel differently these days. In the past, my philosophy was always to try to carry all of your luggage on the plane. However, with all the time needed for security screening, and newer, larger airports with further distances to walk to the terminal, it's a lot easier in most cases to check your big bag and carry on only what you need for the first 24 hours of your trip. Remember when we used to travel this way?

If you are a road warrior traveling for business and have your packing down to a science, by all means, continue to carry-on everything you need. Early boarding and priority seating are just a few of the benefits of being a frequent traveler. Just having the first crack at the overhead compartments feels like a benefit these days.

However, if you're like most travelers, you're not flying first class and you don't usually gaze into an empty overhead bin. And most of us don't have the height and upper body strength to balance a 25 lb. bag over our head and stuff it into that already overcrowded overhead compartment, particularly if we're out of breath from rushing to the gate because we had to stop and open up that bag once — maybe twice — to have its contents inspected. That amount of stress is no way to start a trip, and you can avoid most of it by checking your bags.

Checking a bag is the only way to go if only for this simple reason: You'd like to travel with a pocket knife. In the post 9/11 world, I tried to carry-on with my "carry-on only" philosophy for months after the new restrictions came out, which meant I could not travel with anything sharp. So every time I arrived at my destination I wound up purchasing a pair of tweezers, and living without my little sewing scissors & swiss army knife was a huge challenge. When I realized that I now own 17 pair of tweezers (!), I knew I had to reevaluate that strategy.

As one traveler told me at our travel tips workshop, "With all the airline carry-on restrictions these days the only thing sharp you can take aboard a plane is your wit!" He's right.

Items not permitted in carry-on luggage include: knives, cutting instruments, ice picks, straight razors, metal scissors, metal nail files, corkscrews, baseball bats, golf clubs, pool cues, ski poles & hockey sticks. Rule of thumb, if it's sharp, pointed or could be wielded as a weapon, leave it at home or pack it in your checked bags.

Items currently permitted in carry-on bags include nail clippers, walking canes, umbrellas, safety razors, tweezers & eyelash curlers, however this is always subject to change. It's a good idea to review your airline's list of restrictions shortly before your trip to be certain that you have not packed a newly restricted item, or left out something that is now considered permissible. Some airlines have approved knitting needles and the FAA has approved that item — for now. As a precaution, you can carry a padded self-addressed, stamped envelope in case you place something in your carry-on bag that can't be carried on (knitting needles, etc). Some airports will allow you to mail that item back to yourself or to your destination. Go to www.faa.gov for updates.

Tips

- If you're planning to check luggage, you should arrive at the airport 90 min. before flight departure *(2 hrs. if international)*.

- Travel with two forms of photo ID, just in case you misplace one, you're covered.

- Bring a boarding pass, ticket, or ticket confirmation, such as a printed itinerary, as well as a government-issued photo ID. At most airports, only boarding passes will be accepted to enter the passenger checkpoint.

■ Bring evidence verifying you have a medical implant (or other device) if it is likely to set off the alarm on the metal detector. Keep this information with your tickets. Although this is not a requirement, it may help to expedite the screening process.

■ Choose bags with a single packing space over those with multiple pockets or inside pouches. It makes the process of screening bags through X-ray or hand checks easier.

■ Place everything that you can inside resealable plastic bags. This includes clean & soiled laundry.

■ To prevent delays at the security checkpoint, think about what you're wearing before you leave for the airport. Some larger accessory pieces like belt buckles and shoes or boots with a metal shank in them will set off the alarm and cause you to be searched, which could result in further delay (and maybe missing your flight if you're tight on time).

■ Be prepared to demonstrate that electronic gear works, including laptops, cameras & cell phones.

■ Upon arrival, be sure to go directly to the baggage claim area to claim your luggage. Unfortunately many airports do not have security checking all bag claim tickets and you want to ensure that you're the only one walking out with your bags.

■ Above all, if you are searched, keep your cool & be pleasant.

Some great travel essentials to help you "fly" through airport security:

Luggage Locks
It's ok to lock your bags again, if you use Travel Sentry™ Certified Locks.

The TSA (Transportation Security Administration) now allows you to secure your bag with these special locks. If airport security personnel need to inspect your checked bag, they no longer need to cut your locks or force the bag open and risk damaging it. These new locks allow TSA to open your locks and re-lock your bags, sending them quickly on their way. To order these locks, please go to www.packit-up.com.

Remember: Never pack anything valuable in your checked bag. Always keep valuables with you in your carry-on bag.

Luggage ID

All bags are required to have an ID tag, so be sure to fill out the tags at home so you don't have to do it while standing in line at check-in. You want to make sure you know which bags are yours while going through security and using bright neon luggage tags is the answer. Never put your home address on your luggage ID tag. Please see page 42.

Boarding Pass Holder

This travel essential hangs around your neck like a security badge, but is made specifically to organize your travel documents while you are in the airport. Individualized pockets for your boarding pass, photo ID and passport make it a breeze when you have to show your documents numerous times while juggling your carry-on bags on each leg of your trip. Once at your destination, pack it away until your return trip home. (Tip: Slip a few dollars in for coffee/newspaper/tips for easy access).

TICKETS

PASSPORT

PHOTO ID

Security Wallet

Not to be confused with a Boarding Pass Holder, you wear this wallet under cover packed with items that you don't need access to while you're in the airport such as: traveler's checks, credit cards, etc. Wearing your valuables inside your clothing (except for photo ID),

is not only smart but it is one less thing that
security has to check. Be certain however
not to carry anything metal inside it so
that you won't have to undress just to get
through the first security checkpoint.
Upon arrival, transfer all your items from
your Boarding Pass Holder to your Security
Wallet for safety.

There are many types of security
wallets, however the one I prefer is
the waist wallet: It is large enough
to accommodate airline tickets, etc. And, I
prefer the double zipper wallet for better organization.

Packing Folders & Cubes

Folders are another great way to organize your items, especially dress
shirts & pants. Pack a day's worth of clothing inside each folder to
keep it wrinkle free & easy to inspect. Great for car travel and for
organizing large duffle bags where items tend to get lost at the
bottom of the bag. And the best way to organize all your small,
easy to loose pieces of clothing are packing cubes. They are made
with see-through mesh netting or are plastic which make it easy for
security (and you) to see what's inside each bag without opening it.
Be sure to pack any valuables like cameras or breakables in padded
cubes for added protection while en route.

Compression Bags

Simply put, these are the best kept secret that all travelers need to
know about. You'll help make securities job easier as they can see &
feel what's packed inside each bag without directly touching it.

In addition to keeping all of your items organized, clean &
protected, reusable compression bags will also seal in odors and
moisture, so they're great for dirty laundry on the way home.
Packing bulky items like sweaters in these bags can create up to
75% more space in your bag. (Remember you can also add a great
deal of weight to your bag so be careful how many compression
bags you use!).

Step 1. Packing a Compression Bag

Make sure all articles are folded neatly before placing them in the bag. Make sure all pins or sharp objects are removed from clothing. Slide items into bag.

Step 2. Closing the Zipper

Squeeze sealer and slide from one end to the other. Ensure the zipper is completely closed by zipping it back & forth a few times.

Step 3. Compressing Articles in the Bag

You can either roll or press straight down on the bag to compress and release excess air. To compress by rolling, start at the zipper end and roll towards the valve end. Hold onto packed articles as you roll, keeping them away from the valve end. To help prevent wrinkling, press straight down on wrinkle sensitive items, rather than roll them.

I realized I couldn't travel without compression bags after my trip to Peru. I was packing for both business & vacation and didn't think I had room for both my fleece jacket & my raincoat. So I packed them each into a medium size compression bag, squished out the air, and packed them in my small carry-on bag. Now I always take 2 compression bags packed with bulky items and 2 extras for laundry on the way home.

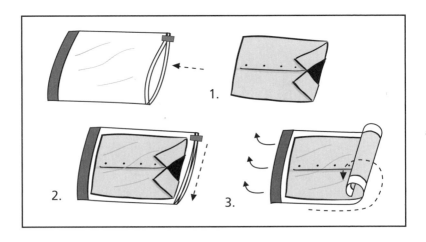

Comfort Items (not just for planes anymore)

A few "must haves" for every carry-on bag: A healthy snack &
a bottle of water. As the saying goes, "You never know when
your next meal is coming". Inflatable neck & lumbar pillows and
earplugs & eyeshades also provide an extra touch of comfort on the
plane. (Tip: Most airlines no longer provide pillows, blankets or
magazines so be prepared & take your own).

Wheeled Tote Bags, Organizers & Computer Bags

Whether you're traveling on vacation or
business, a wheeled carry-on is the perfect solution to large airports. Organize your items in
compression bags & folders and then place
inside your bag to expedite your trip
through security. If traveling with a
computer, be sure your computer is
protected inside a padded computer
case and have it easily accessible for
inspection. Always tape your business
card on your computer in case you're
separated. (Tip: Toss a collapsible tote
bag in for extra purchases along the
way.)

Insiders Tip

Wear clean socks to the airport and shoes that are easy to slip on
and off, in case you have to take your shoes off to go through the
security check.

"If you look like your passport photo,
you're too ill to travel."

Will Kommen

- 4 -
Money, Passports and Other Travel Documents

The most important tip regarding money and documents for a trip is: start early. Too often we hear nightmare accounts of friends forgetting to apply for a passport or visa well in advance and they wind up anxiously awaiting the arrival of the document, hoping their trip will not be in jeopardy.

Depending on your destination, you may need a passport, a visa of some sort or maybe only a driver's license and birth certificate. If you are traveling as part of a tour-group or cruise, visa services may be included as part of your package. Be certain to discuss this with your travel agent as soon as you begin to plan your trip. If you will be responsible for your own documents, it may be worth the extra expense to use a professional passport and visa service to complete the process for you. The last thing you want is to be detained in an airport — where nobody speaks English — because your visa application wasn't processed properly. Please see the resources page at the back of the book for a list of websites with information on how to obtain passports and visa applications.

Once you have your passport, visas, and inoculations, the following suggestions will help you avoid misfortunes along your way.

Security Wallet

The most important thing that you'll pack for any trip is your security wallet. I use mine not only when I travel internationally, but also in large cities and large public events. There are many styles of security wallets, the two most common are those worn around the neck and those worn around the waist. As mentioned earlier, I prefer the type that goes around my waist.

The secret to being comfortable while wearing a security wallet is this: Wear it over an undergarment (not against your skin) and underneath your tucked-in shirt (or beneath the waistband of your pants). Be certain it is never visible. Wearing elastic waisted clothing makes access to a security wallet much easier.

Security Wallet Checklist:

❏ Passport

❏ Drivers License/Photo ID

❏ Immunization records

❏ Travelers checks

❏ Large amounts of cash

❏ 2 major credit cards

❏ Airline/Rail/Bus tickets

❏ Phone/ATM card

❏ Copy of itinerary

❏ Recent pictures of people you're traveling with, especially children

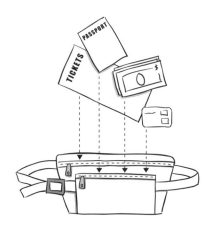

I'm always asked what type of money I prefer to travel with and here's my answer: Everything. I carry travelers' checks, 2 major credit cards, US cash, cash in the currency of the country I'm traveling and an ATM card. Better to be prepared than not.

The reason I travel with 2 major credit cards is: I have been in many situations where a hotel or restaurant will not accept one card, but they will the other. I also pack a photo copy of the front & back of my credit cards just incase I need to call & cancel them, I have all the necessary information.

The Ultimate Day Bag

Here's the solution to the problem of carrying everything you need for the day conveniently: A convertible shoulder/waist bag. Wear it over your shoulder across the front of your body for security in the city (too often women wear their purse hanging behind them which can invite problems) then unzip the side zippers and it converts to a waist pack that you can either wear in front for security or move to the back when you're away from crowds. Black is a good color choice as you can wear it out to dinner in the evening.

Here's the secret: I keep enough cash for the day in this bag for anything I might need like lunch, small souvenirs, museum tickets, etc. (approx. $75 cash). This way, I only need to go into my security wallet for a major purchase or to cash traveler's checks, and I can do this when I'm in a secure location, i.e. at a bank or inside my hotel room.

As well, if by chance this bag is lost or stolen, I'm only out my camera, some money, souvenirs, etc. My passport & valuables are still safely tucked away & secure. By keeping your passport & important documents in a security wallet, it's a safer way to travel in crowded cities and trains.

Tips

- Always photocopy your passport and credit cards before leaving home. Take the copy along with you and keep in a safe place separate from the originals. If the need arises and you need these numbers you can use the photocopies to help you report lost or stolen documents. Also leave a copy at home with someone in case you need it.

- In addition to a photocopy of your passport, also scan your passport ID page into a computer file and mail it to yourself at a web-based email address (hotmail, yahoo, etc.). If you have access to the internet and a printer, you can have access to a copy of your passport.

- Keep airline, travel and personal phone numbers easily accessible in your wallet and move them to an outer pocket of your carry-on when your flight has been canceled or delayed.

- Be sure to always carry your passport with you for ease in cashing traveler's checks.

■ Carry extra passport photos just in case you need them to replace your passport or for additional visas.

■ Super glue a small piece of Ultra Suede to the back side of your passport so it won't slip out of your passport carrier easily. Velcro will also work.

■ Place a small round identifying sticker on the upper right-hand corner of your passport (outside) so it's easier to distinguish when traveling with a group.

■ When traveling in really questionable areas, for extra security, wear two concealed security wallets, one around your neck & one around your waist. In case you're approached & someone demands your money, give them the "fake" wallet which only has a little bit of money in it.

Tips for Traveling with Cash

■ Take a small amount of currency ($75) in the country's local currency for arrival, in case the banks are closed and you need it for porters, taxies, or buses.

■ Call your bank prior to leaving and receive the current exchange rates of the countries you're traveling to. Write them down and keep them in your wallet for quick reference.

■ Don't forget to take a small amount of your own country's currency to use upon departure and arrival from your home city.

■ Carry small amounts of cash (.50 cents to $1.00) for bathroom attendants — a custom of many countries and often is a must to receive toilet paper!

■ Don't flash large amounts of cash in the open.

■ Never carry your wallet in your back pocket.

Tips for Travelers Checks

■ Many small bed & breakfasts and small businesses don't accept credit cards or travelers checks, be sure to confirm in advance.

■ Before buying travelers checks, check into places that may give them to you free: Your own bank, Visa, American Express, AAA, etc.

■ Take travelers checks in both the husband and wife's name for ease in cashing.

■ Share traveler's checks between husband and wife or traveling companions in case of unwanted separation or theft.

■ If traveling to many countries, consider purchasing your travelers checks in smaller denominations, making it easier to use up all the currency before you leave. And when moving from country to country quickly, you don't need to spend as much time converting left-over change.

■ Alternatively, if you will be visiting only a few countries and spending a great deal of money on large purchases, then it would be more sensible and beneficial to obtain travelers checks in large denominations, or consider using a credit card, which may insure the purchase as well.

Tips for Credit Cards

■ Travel only with the major credit cards you plan on using or will need in case of an emergency. Leave all others at home.

■ When traveling with a companion, make sure that each of you takes different credit cards, if they are in the same name. Therefore, if one is lost and you have to cancel it, you will have a back-up card. Also, you will have a higher total credit limit on two cards than on one, just in case you decide to extend your holiday.

■ It's a good idea to carry one credit card separately from the rest in case the others are lost or stolen you'll still have one major credit card.

■ Consider purchasing your airline ticket with a major credit card in case the airline goes under and you lose your money. A credit card company usually has larger resources for such situations so you're not out the money in the meantime.

■ Ask what credit cards are accepted before dining or purchasing something. This saves embarrassing situations.

■ If you are a serious shopper and think that you'll spend everything at the onset of your holiday, consider sending money to designated destinations on your itinerary.

■ If you're traveling in a country which still makes carbon copies of your credit card purchases, be sure to tear up them up. This helps assure that no one can find your credit card number and misuse it.

ATM's

■ Don't forget to take your ATM card as an alternative to traveler's checks & credit cards.

■ Be sure to find out in advance from your bank your numerical/alphabetical PIN number as it differs from country to country and the availability of ATM's.

Customs

■ Keep a list of all the receipts from your purchases for your return home through customs. For ease, record them in your travel journal at the end of each day, and save time by writing once at the end of each day: about your travels and keeping track of expenditures at the same time.

■ While some people consider it a challenge to bring undeclared items through customs, this can be a disastrous and expensive ending to a nice trip.

■ Pack all your purchases in the same piece of luggage in case customs asks to see them. This saves time and embarrassment digging for them.

Tips on Tipping

The first tip I have about tipping is that any guide is just that, a guide. If you receive service that is exceptional (or vice-versa) your tip should reflect that. Be sure to always read the bill carefully, as in many parts of the world, a gratuity has automatically been added.

Keep some small bills in an outside pocket for tips so you don't have to open your wallet at an inconvenient time. If you're giving someone a particularly nice tip, be sure to hand it to them directly. And remember, never tip uniformed personnel. Please see page 114 for cruise ship tipping.

TIPPING GUIDE	
Bellman	$1-$2 per bag
Doorman	$1-$2 per bag
Hotel Maid	$1 per day
Room Service	Usually included in bill
Food Servers	15%-20%
Bartender	15%-20%
Concierge	$5-$10
Coat Check	$1
Sky Cap	$2 per bag
Taxi Drivers	15%-20%
Day Bus Tours	$1-$2

"On a long journey,
even a straw weighs heavy."

Spanish proverb

-5-
Luggage Tips

The most important luggage tip is to check out your luggage long before your holiday to assure that all cases are in working order. Second to you, they will be the most important thing to survive your trip. Most travelers find out the hard way that the first three letters in the word "luggage" spell "lug".

Examine the hinges, wheels, seams, straps, zippers, and especially handles for wear and tear. Most large luggage stores and shoe repair shops can make any necessary repairs.

If you are in the market for new luggage, take into consideration what type of travel you will be doing overall. Ask friends and family what their favorite piece of luggage is and why. And before you purchase your luggage, be sure to lift and carry it or roll it around the store once or twice to see if it's manageable. (If possible, see how it rolls on an escalator for ease in airports and hotels).

Do not buy cheap luggage. The mental anguish is not worth the savings. However, designer luggage will be stolen before old, worn luggage every time, so consider your luggage purchases seriously. Paying extra for designer labels may not be worth it in the long run. A middle-of-the-road purchase is usually the safest bet.

If you have some luggage that is still usable but you'd like to upgrade to a newer bag with better features, here's a suggestion: Donate your used luggage to your favorite charity and treat yourself to a new bag.

When purchasing new luggage, look for wheels, expandable luggage and luggage with self-repairing zippers.

Carry-on & Checked Baggage Guidelines

The most important tip is to call the airline on which you're traveling and find out the most up-to-the-minute baggage allowances for your trip. They do change and the last thing you want to encounter is to have to spend money if your bag is over-sized or overweight.

The following is a guideline of what is allowed on most airlines at the time of printing:

Carry-On Bags Domestic

Most airlines allow one bag and one personal item such as a purse, briefcase, or laptop computer to be carried on the plane. A carry-on bag must fit under your seat or in the overhead bin. Its dimensions should not be more than 9x14x22 (length + height + width) or 45 linear inches (the length, height and width added together).

Airlines may require that a carry-on item travel as checked baggage if the item cannot be safely stowed on a particular flight. Be prepared & know what items you'd need to take out in case this happens to you (i.e. medication, valuables, etc).

The maximum weight allowance for most airlines carry-on bag is 40 pounds, but a maximum weight of 15 pounds for ease in handling is suggested. Again, check with your specific carrier for their allowances as they vary depending on plane structure.

Most airlines exempt the following personal items from the one piece limit:

■ Child safety seats & strollers for ticketed children

■ Assistive devices (i.e. canes, crutches, etc)

■ Outer garments (i.e. coats, hats, etc.)

Checked Bags Domestic

For domestic travel you may check two bags free of charge. The two checked bags may be up to 62 inches (length + width + height) and 50 pounds each.

Generally, you may substitute bowling, fishing, golfing, or skiing equipment for one piece of the two allowable checked pieces. Confirm in advance.

Carry-on Bags International

Generally, international flights are more restrictive than domestic. One carry-on bag up to 45 linear inches and up to 40 pounds & and one small personal bag (i.e. purse) are usually all this is permitted on International flights. This varies greatly from departure city & airline.

Checked Bags International

Size and weight rules vary by destination. Generally, you may check two bags that do not exceed 62 linear inches and 70 pounds each. Contact your airline or your travel agent prior to your trip for details regarding restrictions.

Oversized & Overweight Bags

If your bag is larger or heavier than the linear inches permitted by the airline (add up the total of the width, length & height) you will be charged an additional fee. Get out your measuring tape in advance & step on your bathroom scale with your bag to make sure you're within guidelines.

Excess Baggage

With long check-in lines & more airline baggage restrictions, many travelers are sending their bags ahead via luggage-shipping services. These services will pick up your luggage at your home, office or hotel and deliver it to your destination overnight. An alternative (and less expensive means) is to ship your bag via UPS Ground or the Postal Service. Compare rates and transit times and see what works best for you.

Delayed & Damaged Luggage

Unfortunately, it happens. If your bags don't come off the conveyor belt or are damaged, a report should be filed at the Baggage Service Office immediately before leaving the airport.

My Favorite Bags

1) 22" rolling & expandable bag (24" expandable for longer trips)

2) 16" rolling organizer bag

3) Collapsible zippered tote bag

4) Convertible day bag (shoulder/waist pack)

Depending on the trip, I usually check my large bag (22") and carry-on the other three bags. The secret to being able to carry on three bags is: I pack my purse/day bag inside the collapsible tote which results in having just two bags, one carry-on & one personal.

The reason I have two wheeled bags is that once I check my large bag, I'm stuck without wheels. Most airports are huge, and this way I have a wheeled tote bag which allows me to breeze along the terminals without carrying all that weight on my shoulders.

In transit, I attach the 16" rolling organizer to the 22" rolling bag and place the tote bag (with my day bag inside) on top. This way I'm only rolling one bag behind me & there's no need to search for porters or carts.

Tips

■ Never put your home address on your luggage ID tag. This is a sure way of telling everyone that you are not at home, in case you arrive at your destination and your bag is circling the baggage terminal in another airport. It is not mandatory in all airports to show your baggage claim check upon entering or exiting the baggage terminal, and anyone may have access to your luggage and home address on the tag.

■ Instead, put your travel agent's address and telephone number, a relative, a trusted neighbor, or your office/work number. Of course, leave a detailed copy of your itinerary including hotel addresses with someone you trust. It wouldn't do any good for airport personnel to call your home anyway, as there wouldn't be anyone there to answer!

■ Always place an ID tag on your carry on bag as well.

■ Tie a combination of ribbons on each piece (whether checked or carry on) as well as on your purse/briefcase for easy ID and inclusion with a lost luggage report. Do not use red ribbon only. The majority of black luggage that I see has red ribbons on it.

■ Place a copy of your ID and itinerary inside your luggage in case you are separated from it. This way it stands a chance to catch up with you. Also, tags often are torn off along the way due to frequent handling.

■ Each checked bag must have the name of the person traveling on the outside of the bag.

■ Constantly count your luggage while traveling (including carry-ons, briefcases and purses) to assure that something was not left on the plane, train, bus, taxi, or ship.

■ Before leaving home: take a photo of your luggage (including carry-ons). This photo will serve as a reference in case your luggage is lost and assist with baggage and insurance claims. Quite often travelers are very flustered (understandably) when their luggage is misplaced and forget what they actually brought. Traveling frequently and bringing different bags on various trips can add to the confusion.

■ Remove all old baggage claim tickets from your bags. They are easily confused when traveling, so keep them at home in your scrap book. Remember to remove all carry straps from your luggage before checking it on the plane. They tend to catch on other objects and are quite often damaged or missing when you receive your luggage at the other end.

■ If you're taking sports equipment or other large items with you to the airport, call your airline in advance to find out if there are any additional charges or special packing instructions/restrictions.

■ Use bright luggage straps that clip together to identify your luggage more quickly—then use them again while moving around w/your luggage to "piggy-back" your carry-on or purchases to your roll luggage. Less to carry, easier to handle purchases.

■ The serious shopper should check into expandable suitcases. They can be found in a variety of sizes and styles. Generally, they are soft-sided bags with zippers at the top and bottom. Be sure to check the wheels and the carry straps to assure the bag is strong enough to get it all home.

■ For major shopping holidays, pack a small suitcase with all your items, and then place it inside a large empty suitcase. When you are ready to return home, fill the empty one with your purchases.

■ Pack a lightweight nylon zip bag with shoulder strap for any extra purchases made along the way—and it packs easily. How often have we all needlessly spent money on another bag when our closets are full of them!

■ For lots of souvenirs, pack an extra large collapsible bag in your suitcase. On your return trip, fill it up & it becomes a roomy 22" x 18" x 7" bag that's sturdy enough to use as a checked piece of luggage.

■ Don't forget compression bags to save even more space on the way home.

■ Carry extra keys to your luggage. Combination lock luggage has an advantage over key locks, since you don't have to risk searching for lost keys. As most luggage keys will open luggage of a similar type, ask the hotel or your neighbor for a key if you do forget or lose yours.

■ Use a luggage strap around the girth of your suitcases to keep them securely closed. Be sure to write your name on it in ink to discourage people from taking it along your travel route.

■ For a distinctive luggage tag, try a bone-shaped metal ID tag — found at pet stores. These usually offer more space for information as well.

■ Do not put your title on your luggage tag, for example, Dr., Capt., Prof., etc. This increases your chance for theft.

■ Make an old fashioned "pom-pom" in a bright color yarn to tie on the handle of your luggage. This makes it more personalized and easier for you to identify on the baggage carousel and in large groups of bags.

■ Spray a large "dot" in the center of your case, using a fluorescent color, and no one will want it!

■ Use brightly colored surgical or electrical tape in a unique design or your initials to identify your case and as a deterrent to thieves.

■ Put your initials in the upper right-hand corner of your luggage for added identification. Inexpensive stencils can be purchased at a department store; when so many bags look alike, this will help you identify yours.

■ Do not check your luggage curbside unless it is absolutely necessary. It is best to take it inside to the counter. The ticket counter has up-to-the last minute information of your flight details in case of cancellation or delay.

Luggage Care

■ Nest luggage (place smaller bags inside larger bags) whenever possible to save space.

■ Place crumpled-up newspapers inside luggage to help keep dampness and mildew to a minimum. The paper will absorb the wetness. Change every few months.

■ When storing luggage, dampness can be a problem, so putting some small packets of silica gel (that come in shoe boxes) can be very useful to ward away dampness in stored luggage, camera bags, shoe-storage bags, etc.

■ If dampness occurs in luggage, use a hairdryer to eliminate it. Also to cut down on dampness, cut a deodorant bar of soap in half and place inside your luggage during storage.

■ Cedar shavings or kitty litter are also suggested for stored luggage.

■ Place a few dryer sheets inside each bag. This keeps them smelling fresh and clean.

■ If your luggage has been stored for quite awhile, place it open in the sunshine to air it out before packing.

■ To clean your luggage: Use a small hand vacuum cleaner or whisk to clean the inside of your cases. The small size allows you to get into the corners.

■ Remove stains from luggage fabric immediately with soap and water to avoid odor later when damp. When you return home, the bag can be professionally cleaned at either a dry cleaner's or luggage shop. Check the manufacturer's label prior to using any cleaning solution. Water-repellent sprays work wonders on soft-sided luggage to prevent stains and keep water from soaking in.

■ Spend a few moments finding which keys belong to which suitcases. Once you have them together, use twist ties from the kitchen to secure them to the proper handle.

■ Pack off-seasoned clothing inside unused luggage, store in normal room temperature conditions.

Luggage Insurance

There are various ways to insure luggage; check with your travel agent first and find out how much your luggage is insured by your airline or the tour company you are traveling with. If you are traveling on your own, or are interested in additional luggage insurance, here are some options.

■ Inquire into your homeowner's coverage, which generally covers your personal belongings up to an amount stated in your policy, including cameras and luggage.

■ Ask your travel agent to recommend a travel insurance policy. They usually have a few to choose from, with varying amounts of coverage at varying fees.

■ If you charge your air, tour or cruise tickets with certain major credit cards, occasionally you are automatically covered, at no extra charge, against loss or significant damage to your baggage when traveling with a large carrier company (plane, bus, train, or ship). Confirm your card benefits, as they are subject to change.

More Great Tips

■ If you are taking a soft sided suitcase, consider putting all your clothing in plastic bags first. You never know when someone else's bag might break and leak perfume all over your bag.

■ Carry your film in your carry-on baggage. Checked luggage may receive a much more concentrated screening from the high tech scanners, which can ruin film.

"Take half the clothes and
twice the amount of money
you think you'll need."

Unknown

-6-
Planning Your Travel Wardrobe

Choosing a travel wardrobe of basics will help you deal with space limitations. Build your wardrobe using one or two basic colors, so the same shoes, hosiery and accessories can be worn with everything. Some versatile color combinations are black and red, navy and red, brown and beige or black and white.

Simple, classic styles for dress and casual wear usually work best. Make sure that each item of clothing can be worn at least two ways.

For warmer climates, pack lighter colors and natural fabrics, such as cotton. Unlike synthetics, cotton breathes. For cooler climates, dark colored clothing which can be layered for warmth is a good choice. Wool gabardine is a good fabric to travel with as it's light-weight, warm and wrinkle resistant.

One of my favorite items to travel with is a pair of khaki pants because they're the color of — dirt! By wearing dark colors on the bottom, like khaki & black, you don't have to worry about dirt showing as much when you sit on a park bench or on a train seat. The best thing about khaki is that any color in the world matches it. That takes out half the stress of planning what to wear! And, depending on my destination, I also travel with Capri pants or a longer length skirt which helps me blend in and be more culturally sensitive in certain areas of the world.

One clothing question I'm asked more than any other is: How do you pack for changing climates especially when you're starting out in, say, Scandinavia & ending your trip in Greece? The secret is: Layering. You can take items off as you get hot & layer them back on as you get cold. For those travelers who tend to get cold easily: Lightweight long underwear, available in two piece sets (nylon/ cotton or silk) fits well under any type of clothing; they're easy to pack, drip dry overnight and keep you warm. You can even use them for pajamas.

For plane travel, wear loose-fitting clothing with elastic waistbands and comfortable rubber soled shoes for walking long distances in airports. Wear a short sleeved shirt under a long sleeved sweater so if you are arriving to a warmer climate than which you left, you can simply take off the layers as needed. And, don't forget that what you are wearing is an entire day's outfit as well as all the clothes that you have packed so make sure these items mix & match with your packed clothes.

Organizing your wardrobe is easier if you have a list of things that you plan to take with you. Keep the list of items in your carry-on bag. If checked bags are misplaced, the list of contents can help identify them.

I pack almost the same amount of clothes for a one week trip as I do for a three week trip. I just wash along the way (see page 87). Who wants to carry their entire closet around on vacation?

Shoes

Shoes are always a hot topic. At one of our seminars a woman suggested we form a self-help group for women who travel with too many shoes and another woman suggested that I have seminar participants sign a contract that they wouldn't pack more than 3 pairs of shoes!

Through out the years, I've definitely found there are "shoe people" in this world that have to travel with every pair of shoes that they own. If you're one of them, and you just can't convert, be sure you have someone available to help you carry your bags.

My suggestion is to travel with a maximum of 3 pairs of shoes, one that you're wearing and two that you pack. My preference is a good walking shoe, a comfortable dressy loafer and a pair of sandals. Modify your shoes depending on your destination and be sure to break in any new shoes before leaving home.

Don't forget to pack rubber-soled shoes for travel that includes cobblestone streets & marble floors where it's easy to slip and fall.

Jewelry

I can't stress this tip enough: Leave your good jewelry safe at home in a locked safety deposit box & take inexpensive jewelry that you can wear without worry. Faux pearls make a very elegant statement and look just as nice as real ones without the worry.

■ Here's how to pack a necklace so it doesn't get kinks in it: Thread it through a straw (cut to the length of the necklace and/or bracelet) and then close the clasp. Place in a travel toothbrush holder so it won't be crushed in your luggage. Pack inside a shoe for further protection.

■ Pack pierced earrings in a lipstick container so they don't get crushed (or use an empty film canister or prescription pill bottle).

■ Pack your jewelry in a mini size double-sided tackle box when traveling. The individual compartments (which can be lined with skid proof shelf lining) work great for earrings and rings. In the longer compartments, put straight pins in the shelf lining at an angle then loop your necklaces around the pins so the chains don't get tangled.

■ If you must take valuables with you, be sure to store them in a hotel/ship safe.

On the next two pages you'll find the Women's and Men's Travel Wardrobe List to get you started. Modify each accordingly, depending on the type of travel that you are doing.

Women's Basic Travel Wardrobe

- ❏ Walking shoes
- ❏ Flat loafers
- ❏ Sandals (if appropriate)
- ❏ Dress shoes (if appropriate)
- ❏ Socks
- ❏ Underwear
- ❏ Hosiery/Slip
- ❏ Pajamas
- ❏ 2 pair of pants, one lighter one dark
- ❏ 2 belts (one in each basic color)
- ❏ Skirt
- ❏ Jacket to match pants and skirt
- ❏ Lightweight sweater
- ❏ Shorts (if appropriate)
- ❏ 3 short sleeved knit t-shirts
- ❏ 2 long sleeved knit t-shirt
- ❏ Evening blouse
- ❏ Dress (if appropriate)
- ❏ Swimsuit/Pareo
- ❏ Costume jewelry
- ❏ Scarf
- ❏ Raincoat
- ❏ Hat/gloves (if appropriate)
- ❏ Travel umbrella (if appropriate)
- ❏ Athletic wear (if appropriate)
- ❏ Convertible handbag = day into evening

Men's Basic Travel Wardrobe

- ❏ Walking shoes
- ❏ Thongs or sandals
- ❏ Loafers or dress shoes
- ❏ Underpants
- ❏ Undershirts
- ❏ Socks (casual)
- ❏ Socks (dress)
- ❏ 2 pair pants
- ❏ Shorts
- ❏ 2 long sleeved shirts
- ❏ 3 Short sleeved shirts (polo and t-shirts)
- ❏ V-neck or crew neck sweater
- ❏ Sport coat
- ❏ Necktie (if appropriate)
- ❏ 2 belts
- ❏ Sleepwear
- ❏ Overcoat
- ❏ Travel umbrella
- ❏ Pair swim trunks (if appropriate)
- ❏ Hat/gloves (if appropriate)
- ❏ Athletic wear (if appropriate)

Travel Wardrobe Planner

The key to an organized travel wardrobe is planning. A few weeks before your trip, start a list of clothing that you'd like to take. Match each piece to a day of travel, then figure out what can be mixed & matched to cut down on what you take. Remember, you can wear each item at least a few times, especially black pants & khaki shorts.

On the facing page you'll find one of my favorite secrets: My *Travel Wardrobe Planner*. I've used this for years and it really works to help cut back on the number of clothes I pack. I started using it for cruises and now I use it for every trip. Please see page 105 for the Cruise Wardrobe Planner.

To help you get started: Add or subtract days on the planner depending on the length of your trip. Write down an outfit for day & night and decide how often you can wear the same things again. Be sure to write down the separate pieces, i.e. black skirt, red blouse, to remind you that separates can be mixed and matched and worn more than one time. Separates stretch your travel wardrobe further than a single item like a dress. You'll be amazed at how much less you'll really need to take (and how much money you can save on things you probably won't wear or need).

Note any events & activities you'll be participating in so you have the appropriate clothing.

Please feel free to make copies so you have extra planners ready for future trips.

Pack It Up—Travel Wardrobe Planner

	City	Daytime Outfit	Evening Outfit	Special Events & Activities
Day 1				
Day 2				
Day 3				
Day 4				
Day 5				
Day 6				
Day 7				

©Pack It Up

Tips

■ Remember to take items that can double for other uses: a raincoat can act as a blanket on a train or bus. A large t-shirt can be used for a nightgown, exercising, or cover-up.

■ Don't overlook the need for some real casual clothes like your favorite sweats, t-shirts, and tennis shoes. These are great for relaxing around the hotel room, exercising, or for long traveling days.

■ Don't forget to pack some dryer sheets. You can use them to de-static knit skirts and tops simply by rubbing them against them. In dry climates, you can rub your comb across them to reduce static in your hair (or even rub them on your head!) Packed in your luggage, they can make your clothes smell nice. Be sure not to use on silk items.

■ Here's an odd tip but some travelers love it: Cut and save the top part of panty hose after the runs make them un-wearable. You can then discard them after use as underwear, leaving a bit more room for souvenirs.

■ When traveling for a special event (i.e. wedding, etc.) or for different climates within one trip pack up the additional clothing, shoes, etc. that are no longer needed and mail them back home once the event is over.

■ You can bring less with you if you plan to purchase some of your wardrobe along the way in the form of souvenir t-shirts & sweatshirts. But be certain that you save enough room in your luggage to bring them home.

■ Convertible clothing extends your travel wardrobe options without the added weight of another piece of clothing. Convertible pants zip off to make an extra pair of shorts and a fleece jacket with zip off sleeves converts to a vest in case the weather warms up.

■ Reversible clothing also stretches your travel wardrobe by giving you two items in one: Check travel catalogs for some great ideas from dresses & skirts, to tank tops and cardigans.

■ Pack some clothes that are on their last legs i.e. underwear or a sweater that's quite worn. During your travels, leave them behind with a note in your hotel room explaining that you've meant to leave it & you've made space for some souvenirs.

"He who would travel happily
must travel light."

Antoine De Saint-Exupery
(1900-1944)

-7-
Pack It In

There is such a wide spectrum of travel these days that you need to tailor your packing to fit your travel needs. Packing wisely can save unnecessary problems and expenses. Be sure to pack lightly, and only pack what you can carry for one mile without putting it down!

Always start with a check list. To save you time, please see page 145 for the **Ultimate Traveler's Checklist.** This checklist covers just about everything you might possibly need for any trip. It is not a checklist of everything you should take for every trip.

This list will help remind you of things that you might need on a particular trip. It will speed up packing and let you know what you might be missing and help you eliminate items that you know you won't need.

The last thing any traveler wants to do is have to buy something on their trip (usually for a lot more that it would normally cost) that they have sitting at home. Feel free to tear out this check-list & make as many copies as you need. It's also posted at **www.packitup.com.**

Packing Your Carry-On Bag

As mentioned in the Luggage Tips chapter, I suggest traveling with a 16" rolling carry-on bag. The reason is that by the time you pack everything you need into your carry-on, it can be incredibly heavy. However, you should also have with you (in an easily accessible place) a collapsible tote bag. The benefit of having the additional bag is that if the airline won't permit you to carry-on your rolling organizer, you can transfer your most important items from your rolling bag to your tote bag and check the rolling bag. You'll also have an extra bag for packing souvenirs in for the trip home.

Following are two checklists. You'll notice that items are divided into a) most important in your personal bag and b) less important in your carry-on bag. In the event you have to check your carry-on bag at the last minute (this happens a lot on smaller aircraft), you will still have everything you need for your flight easily accessible under the seat in front of you.

And remember: Pack as many items as possible in your carry-on bag in plastic bags. This makes everything easier to identify, and you can efficiently transfer any valuable items in a hurry to be kept with you at all times. (see pages 75-79 for plastic bag ideas)

Most importantly, if you are traveling on business or for a special occasion and you must be dressed appropriately, be sure to either wear what you need or carry it on the plane with you. No worries over delayed luggage.

If traveling with a security wallet, please refer to the checklist on page 32 for a list of items to be kept in your security wallet.

Carry-on Checklist Personal Bag:

❏ Document organizer including:
   • Travel documents/Photo ID
   • Credit cards/Cash
   • Travelers Checks

❏ Medications
❏ Jewelry
❏ Camera/film
❏ Computer
❏ Business files
❏ Cell phone
❏ Eye glasses
❏ Keys
❏ Address book

❏ Healthy snack & Water

❏ Tissues

❏ Comfort items (please see page 29)

Carry-on Checklist Rolling Organizer:

❏ Extra reading material

❏ Make-up/toothbrush & paste

❏ Toiletry kit

❏ Change of underwear/socks/shirt

❏ Any item from above list that's not vital to you

Packing Your Suitcase

Interlayering is the name given to the following method of packing either soft-sided or hard-sided luggage and is the most successful in preventing wrinkles in your clothes. Begin with your suitcase open on a flat surface.

1. Place your shoes in pairs with the toe-tucked-in the heel method inside plastic bags. Put your shoes and all heavy items along the bottom of the suitcase (near the hinges). Place belts along the perimeter of the case and heavy items, such as hairdryer, cosmetic case, etc. in the center.
Pack squishable items like underwear and socks around the corners and in between heavy items.

Now place a packing divider on top of these items. If you don't have a packing divider, you can use an over-sized placemat.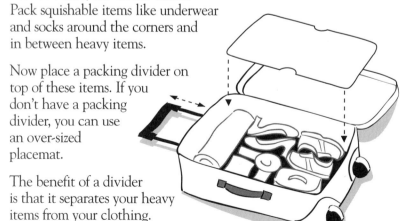

The benefit of a divider is that it separates your heavy items from your clothing.

2. Fold your slacks
   along their natural
   creases and place
   the waistband
   against one edge
   of your suitcase
   with the bottom of the
   pant extending over the
   opposite edge of the case.
   Place the second pair of
   slacks in the same method
   in the opposite direction.

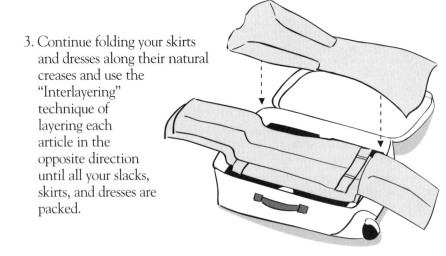

3. Continue folding your skirts
   and dresses along their natural
   creases and use the
   "Interlayering"
   technique of
   layering each
   article in the
   opposite direction
   until all your slacks,
   skirts, and dresses are
   packed.

4. Next, button all jackets, blazers, and long sleeved shirts and pull a dry-cleaner bag over them. Place them in the suitcase with the sleeves being brought in on top of the jacket along their natural creases. The bottom of these items will extend over the top edge of the case.

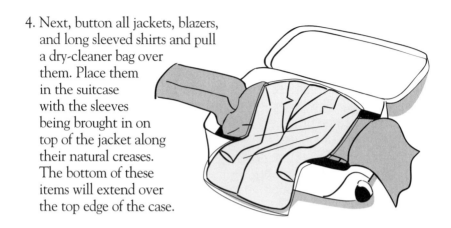

5. Roll up all knit items and place them on top of the layered clothing, leaving the original articles extended over the edges of the case. Make sure you utilized every inch of space so items will not slip during travel

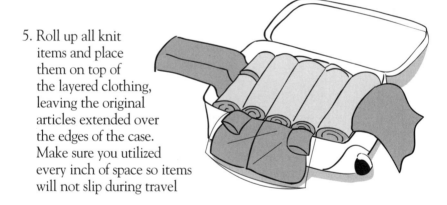

6. When you have utilized every inch of space, bring the ends up & over the rolled items inside the case, alternating sides as you go. This keeps your clothing in a continuous rounded shape without getting wrinkles at the knee caps of the slacks and jacket waistlines. It is also easier to pull out certain items you may need without disturbing the entire case of clothes.

When all items are packed, the benefit of having the packing divider in the middle of the suitcase is that you can reach in and lift out the entire top layer of your packed items without disturbing them and retrieve items on the bottom half of the suitcase. (or add items to the bottom half that you might have forgotten to pack).

Review

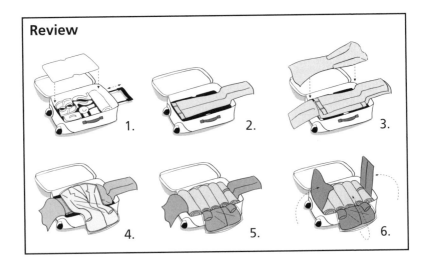

How To Roll Up a T-shirt:

1. Place your t-shirt on a flat surface

2. Fold sleeves to the back

3. Roll up from the bottom.

Remember, the tighter you roll your knits, the less they wrinkle.

1.

Additional Hints For Packing Your Suitcase

■ Begin packing with three sizes of resealable bags next to your bag. Everything that's possible to pack in a bag, do. This not only keeps items more organized but you have extra bags ready if you need them while traveling.

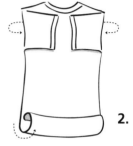

2.

3.

■ Pack all of your heavy items (hairdryer, shoes, electrical converter, etc) on the bottom of your bag. Stuff your shoes with socks, hose, under wear, anything that won't wrinkle easily. Don't forget that you can cover your shoes by pulling a sock over the outside of them.

■ An oldie but a goodie: Place tissue paper between folds.

■ For packing pleated skirts, turn them inside out, wrap masking tape around the hem (to keep the pleats set), and pull into an old pair of panty hose with the top and bottom cut off. This will keep the pleats in and the skirt from wrinkling. Place around the perimeter of case.

■ Roll your outfits together if they are knits. They won't wrinkle and you won't have to search for all your accessories. Add matching socks and underwear.

■ Sweaters are easy to roll up, usually don't wrinkle, and fit well into the corners, thus keeping other items from shifting in your suitcase.

■ When using dry-cleaner bags, make sure that the bag does not have anything printed on it (i.e. advertising). The ink can rub off on clothing when it gets warm.

■ Turn all sequin items or embroidered clothes inside out and place in either a plastic bag or pillowcase to minimize rubbing and loosening sequins. (This also allows you to have your own pillowcase on your trip.)

■ Pack your jewelry in your evening bag so you know exactly where it is and with which outfit you plan to wear it in case you're in a hurry.

■ Stuff all the corners in your luggage with small, soft items to save space: socks, underwear, hose, and all things that won't wrinkle.

■ Fold blouses and men's shirts inside out so the wrinkles are facing inside and not so prominent.

■ Place items that you intend to use first on the top of your suitcase: shorts, bathing suit, pajamas, etc.

■ When packing a bathing suit with cups (or bras) the cups can get crushed. Pack a pair of socks in the cups to keep them filled out. Roll-up and place in a plastic bag to avoid snags.

■ The contents of a suitcase will settle, leaving more space for additional items if packed the day before departure. Pre-packing allows peace of mind and time to clear out that refrigerator.

■ Place men's cufflinks and studs in plastic or felt containers and put in jacket pockets. If valuable, pack in carry-on.

Packing Your Garment Bag

There are many different types and sizes of garment bags on the market. Some have built-in frames and some are simply heavy material designed to cover your clothes. Depending on the specific type of garment bag you have, the following suggestions will assist you in packing it more successfully for your next trip.

When packing your garment bag, use a maximum number of three hangers. Begin by placing your garment bag on a flat surface. Next, layer your clothes on the hangers in the following methods:

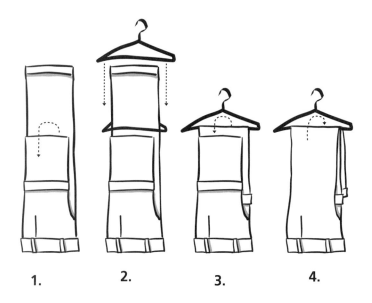

1.   2.   3.   4.

1. Place pants on a flat surface and fold top pant leg back in half

2. Slip hanger on bottom pant leg to knee

3. Fold bottom pant leg to crotch over the hanger

4. Fold top pant leg over the hanger and the other pant leg

This method secures the pants to the hanger without needing clothes pins or safety pins.

(also great for RV travel, car travel, and your home closet!)

1. After securing pants as described, place shirts (buttoning articles as you go along) over the pants and ultimately jackets. Cover each hanger with dry-cleaner bags once all the clothes have been hung on it.

1.

2. Place dresses on the next hanger and cover them with dry-cleaner bags helping to protect them and keep wrinkles to a minimum.

3. After you have all your clothes on the hangers, place your coat (or robe) around all of the clothing, and button it up.

2.   **3.**

Place bundled hanging items inside your garment bag.

Gently fold any garments up at the bottom if they are longer than the garment bag. Secure the strap of the garment bag around the center of the "bundle" if provided.

In the additional packing area around the hangers, stuff the corners with either socks or shoes or knit clothes that have been rolled up. Be sure to pad high-heeled shoes or any sharp items so as not to poke through the bag. Remember, any sharp items must be packed in your checked bag.

The biggest mistake most people make when they pack garment bags is that they don't pack enough to keep items from shifting and everything falls to the bottom of the bag.

Additional Hints for Packing A Garment Bag

■ Use rubber bands to keep hangers together if they are not those that originally came with the bag. This will keep them from falling and snagging clothes on the way down.

■ Place those garments that wrinkle easily at the back of the bag (closest to the outside). In this way, they will have less pressure and be less likely to wrinkle. Don't over pack your garment bag or it will be very cumbersome to carry.

■ Don't forget luggage straps that are used mainly around the girth of hard sided luggage. These are terrific to keep your garment bag together, especially when you're carrying it.

■ Be sure to secure the hook inside your bag by either snapping it in the original closing or by using a piece of string or a twist-tie. (A porter once said that the best way to guarantee you'll never see your bag again is to have it hook one of them as they transfer it.)

■ Place plastic cable ties on your checked garment bag to help keep zippers closed on outside pockets of your bag.

■ When checking a garment bag at the airport, ask at the ticket counter for a cardboard box to help protect it. Most airlines provide these free of charge; they help keep your bag looking new.

■ When carrying your garment bag on the plane, make sure to keep it near your seat. Most often, the closets are filled and it must be stored in the overhead compartment. Tri-fold garment bags are much easier to fit in the overhead compartment (and through security check points).

■ Don't pack valuables in your garment bag in case it is moved out of sight.

Packing A Duffel Bag

When traveling by car, duffels are a great way to organize, especially for family travel. However, it is one of the most difficult bags to pack, unless you know the secrets.

First, always pack a duffel bag on a hard surface. This will help distribute the weight evenly. Next, pack your duffel in layers with the heaviest items on the bottom such as shoes, sandals, extra travel guides and umbrella.

Next, pack your toiletry kit on top of your shoes, which helps protect the contents in case it's dropped. Now pack your clothes. Begin by placing bulky items such as jackets or sweaters, rolled-up on either end, which helps fill-in the corners & protects the items on the inside of the duffel.

Pack the rest of your clothes as previously instructed for a suitcase using a packing divider, however, place the divider on a flat surface like your bed, not inside your duffel. Layer your clothes on top of the divider just like the suitcase packing, and when you're finished you can pick up the entire bundle and place inside your duffel bag.

Stuff your socks, underwear, swim suit, etc. all around the edges of the duffel and remember to never pack anything breakable in a duffel bag.

Another option of packing clothing in a duffel bag, are the packing folders & packing cubes. Build your layers with the packing folders & cubes on top of the bottom layer of shoes.

Finally, pack your rain jacket and pajamas on top next to the zipper, in case they're needed in a hurry. The outside pockets of duffel bags are perfect for packing extra plastic bags and other non-breakable items.

General Packing Tips

■ First, make a list of all the items that you want to take with you as you think of them. Check off these items as you pack. Keep this packing list and use it as a reference for your next trip.

■ Another idea is to list all the activities that you will be at tending while you are away. Now, list what clothes and accessories you need. Start by laying out your items on an extra bed or couch as you think of them.

■ Inter-pack your luggage with your traveling companion: Just in case one piece is missing or delayed, you will still have a few items of your own. This idea also applies to traveling alone and "scattering" your casual, informal, and formal clothes between your various cases. Some may find this impractical, but it works!

■ Women's shoes pack very neatly inside men's shoes. This saves space & the women's shoes are nicely protected. First pack socks and hose inside women's shoe, place women's shoe inside a plastic bag, and then slide women's shoe into man's.

■ Place shoes inside the plastic bag that your newspaper comes in. They are long & perfect for large shoes, and clear so you can see what's inside. Plastic bags from sub sandwich shops also work great.

■ If you run out of plastic bags on your way home, use the complimentary shower cap as a shoe cover (works great on large mens shoes).

- Place all your clothes for the trip out then place half of them back in the closet.

- When in doubt, leave it out!

- Only pack what you can carry around your block without putting down, or for one mile. This gives you a good idea of what you will encounter in an airport without porters.

- If you're pressed for space, wear your heaviest clothing instead of packing it.

- Don't forget the old trick of hanging wrinkled items in a bathroom full of steam to help refresh them.

- Pack paper back books which you plan to read on the trip around the edge of your suitcase for extra protection, and plan to discard (or leave in hotel room) extras as you read them.

- Be sure to pack an outfit in your carry-on bag so that if the worst happens and your checked bag is delayed, you don't have to run out in the middle of the night looking for clothes in a foreign city. Consider this your survival kit of sorts.

- Leave clothes on the wire hangers that come from the cleaners and pack them in your large checked suitcase. This way when you unpack for an extended stay you just lift out the hangers and your clothes are ready to go into the closet.

- Save the inserts of perfume and cologne samples from magazines and your monthly bills to use when traveling. You won't have to worry about bottles breaking.

- Place dryer sheets in between some of the layers of your clothes. This helps keep static cling away & keeps everything smelling fresh. And you have some dryer sheets if you need them for laundry on the road.

- Always remember when packing your bags to pack your respect for people of different cultures. You will most often find that people through out the world are happy to have you as a visitor — as long as you are considerate of them and their way of life.

■ The more your travel, the less you take.

■ Don't forget to pack your patience & your sense of humor.

"The only aspect of our travels that is guaranteed to hold an audience is disaster."

Martha Gellman b.1908

-8-
Plastic Bags to The Rescue

Out of the kitchen and into your bag, don't leave home without resealable plastic bags. Since my first trip to Europe over 26 years ago, and 65 countries later, my favorite packing essential is still the plastic bag. They are my favorite for two reasons: Because they are leak proof and air tight. Additional benefits of traveling with plastic bags include: They are affordable to replace for each trip, you can usually pick some up along the way and you can recycle them.

Before I actually start packing my bags, I first put everything I can inside a plastic bag. The see through feature of packing in plastic makes finding things simple. And the wide variety of sizes—snack, quart, gallon and 2 gallon — allows me to keep the things that I want together, regardless of how big or small they are.

The plastic is great for separating wet items, like swimsuits and exercise clothes, and the 2 gallon size are perfect for laundry that you don't want to think about until you get home!

And don't forget to pack extra's for use along the way & the trip home: Make your own "soft pack" of varying sizes of plastic bags to travel with. Pack quart & snack size bags inside a gallon bag & pack gallon bags inside 2 gallon bags. (The gallon bags don't fit well into themselves!). Roll up and secure with a rubber band or pack flat on the bottom of your bag.

Distribute extra bags through-out your luggage; inside your toiletry kit, in the outside pockets of your carry-on, inside your pockets of your luggage, etc. You'll find uses for them everywhere. Even pack one in your coat pocket — just in case!

Airport Organization with Plastic Bags

Security Organizer

As mentioned in Packing Smart for Airport Security, pack every-thing you can in your carry-on in a plastic bag first. Not only will this help expedite your trip through security because they're see-through, it will help organize your bag. And why not make it as pleasant as possible for security personnel: Keep personal items like under wear inside a plastic bag.

Here's a tip: Start emptying your pockets before you get up to the security check point. Keep a plastic bag in your carry-on for just this purpose.

Sharps!

Write "Sharps" on the outside of a quart size bag so you remember to pack everything together that isn't permitted in your carry-on bag. Always pack this bag in your checked-in bag. (Your pocket knife, cork screw, scissors, any sharp item).

Film

Always place your film inside a plastic bag before you pack it in your carry-on bag. This will help expedite the screening process if you request a hand inspection of your film at security. (The bag allows the inspector to view the canisters easily). Be sure to arrive early to avoid long lines and remember: Never pack film in your checked luggage. Equipment used for screening checked baggage might damage your undeveloped film.

Valuable Bag

Keep valuables (or any necessary items like medicine) together in a plastic bag that you can pull from your carry on, should you have to check your carry-on at the last minute for any reason.

Plane Pocket

Keep all your items close at hand on the plane by organizing them in a "plane pocket". Pack everything you'll need on your plane trip inside a gallon size bag: Healthy snack, comfort items, CD player, medication, pens & paper, paperback, glasses etc. and place in the seat pocket in front of you. You won't loose items as easily. Place inside a mesh laundry bag so you can't see through it and to add durability.

Healthy Food on The Go

You can take it with you, so why not? Fill-up some small snack size bags with healthy snacks for your trip. Here are some ideas: Dried cranberries, beef jerky, mixed nuts, carrots & celery and trail mix. Combined with a small bottle of water, you've got a meal on the go.

More Great Travel Tips with Plastic Bags

Scrapbook Organizer — Travel Memories

When traveling to numerous countries on one trip, write each country (i.e. Italy) on the front of a gallon size bag & organize your mementos accordingly. When you return home, it's a breeze to put your scrapbook in order. Toss in your souvenir coins, museum tickets (some are works of art), brochures and postcards in the correct "country".

Personal Care Organizers

Arrive at your destination organized by grouping your personal care items by category inside plastic bags. Pack all the items you use in the shower like shampoo, conditioner, soap, razor, etc. in a gallon size bag and mark the outside shower. For items you use by the bed, like alarm clock, lotion, tissues, write bedside on the bag. Make a few sink bags, one containing make-up & cotton swabs, one containing deodorant, facial cleanser, moisturizer, and yet another containing your toothbrush, toothpaste & floss. Pack all these bags inside your hanging toiletry kit (packed with your brush, etc) for traveling.

Travel Make-up Kit

Always pack each individual cosmetic item inside a plastic bag. Keep a box of snack size bags in your bathroom cupboard, handy for every time you pack your makeup. Just in case your foundation leaks en route, it won't ruin your expensive blush. Pack all your individually bagged makeup inside a quart size bag (or gallon size if needed!).

Comfort on the Go

After a long day of travel (or sightseeing) you might have a few sore muscles. Soak a wash cloth in warm water & place inside a plastic bag to make a hot compress. Alternatively, make a cold compress by placing ice in a bag. To avoid leaks, double-up your bags. The hot compress idea is also good to use as a hot water bottle in a pinch—place in your bed a few minutes before retiring & warm up your sheets!

Car Organization

Organize everything from your glove compartment to your trunk with extra strong plastic bags. Pack maps, flashlight, etc. and keep close at hand. Keep your insurance card, car ID, etc. all together in a quart size bag, just in case. Keep children's small snacks, games, and drawing all together in a gallon bag in the backseat pocket, with-in their reach.

Use 2 gallon bags to keep awkward sized items like flares & jumper cables contained. For winter weather keep one packed with warm gloves, hat & socks. For the summer, keep one packed with sunscreen, extra bathing suit & sun hat (one for each child). These fit easily under the front seats.

Luggage/Clothing Organization

Gallon size bags are great for children's clothing. Pack an entire day's worth of clothes inside a gallon bag & write each child's name on the outside. This is a great way to organize a duffle bag or a suitcase. The 2 gallon size bags work well for adult-sized items like bulky sweaters, coats & shoes (and you can also pack a day's worth of clothes inside).

Directions: Fold the items an inch smaller than the bag & stack on top of each other. Then, slide the entire stack of clothes into the bag on a flat surface and press ALL air out of the bag. Close zipper until one inch remains open. Press remaining air out of the bag and zip the bag all the way closed. Toss in your suitcase. This makes a very flat package & takes up less room in your luggage. To reduce wrinkles & save space, try to remove as much air as possible and flatten with your hands.

Travel Washing Machine
Save money on laundry by turning a plastic bag into a washing machine. See page 88.

Garbage Bags
Grab a few large garbage bags from under your kitchen sink before you head out on your next trip. From a drop cloth for a picnic to an impromptu rain poncho you'll be prepared. Cover your luggage if it's raining or line the inside of your luggage to protect your clothing, just in case it's left out in the rain.

Compression Bags
The ultimate plastic bag, the compression bag is great for a variety of items. My favorite use is for dirty laundry. Since they seal in odors and moisture, they're also great for wet swimsuits and damp workout gear. They are also wonderful for packing fleece jackets, sweaters, and entire outfits. And, for anyone who likes to travel with their own pillow, you can actually pack a full size pillow into a large compression bag & shrink it down to less than 1". Please see pages 27-28.

"A vacation is what you take
when you can no longer take
what you've been taking."

Earl Wilson b.1907

-9-
Packing Your Toiletries

Packing toiletries and other personal care items can be the most challenging part of packing for many travelers. Figuring out the best way to prevent leaks and even deciding exactly what to bring along can be difficult.

The first place to start is to use a good toiletry kit. You want to separate your personal care items from everything else in your bag just in case something leaks. And you need this bag to be multi-functional, so it fits any type of travel you're going to do.

My hanging toiletry kit has traveled the world with me and suits my needs well. I've used the same one for over 10 years, from 5 star cruises to trekking in Nepal.

The reason I like it so much is: The hook allows me to hang the bag on any door handle, shower rod or towel rack, which is a great benefit when there's limited counter space.

It's large enough for all my toiletries, including shampoo, conditioner, hair brush, toothbrush/paste, etc. It also has a non breakable removeable mirror.

Be sure to pack your toiletries one to two days in advance and then go through your normal routine. Check to make sure that everything you need is ready to go. Remember that trial sizes of everything save space.

More great tips for organizing your personal care items

■ If you go on frequent trips, keep it packed so you're always ready to go.

■ A great time saver: Keep a list of items in your toiletries bag that are running low when you're traveling. As soon as you return,

stock the bag relying on your list to prepare for the next trip.
Then all you have to do is grab it out of the closet and go. No
need for that mad dash to the store for last minute items.

■ The luggage compartment of a plane is not pressurized &
changes in pressure make liquids expand, causing leaks. When
packing liquids for air travel, help prevent leaks by making sure
each bottle is only filled 3/4 of the way full with liquid. Then,
squish out all the air and screw on the lid. That way, the liquid
has room to expand. Use a plastic bag as back-up.

■ Place a small piece of plastic wrap over the lid of your bottles
before closing. This keeps the liquid from spilling.

■ Purchase leak-proof plastic bottles at luggage stores or travel
catalogs which are much better than the empty plastic bottles
found at drug stores which often leak. Nalgene® bottles are the
favorite of experienced travelers.

■ Bottles with a spray pump never really seal completely and
may leak. Remove the spray pump and transfer the liquid to a
leak proof bottle, bringing the travel sized spray pump bottle
separately. Assemble once you're at your destination.

■ Contact lens wearers should carry their spare glasses, a lens case
and a small bottle of saline with them in their carry on, as long
flights can dry and irritate the eyes.

■ Shop periodically for trial size items you know you will
eventually need, and put them away for your upcoming trip.
No need to spend time decanting large bottles to small ones.

■ Ever reach into your toiletry kit & cut yourself on your razor?
Retractable razors are the answer. ($5) The head twists into itself
& your can purchase replacement blades from the drugstore.

■ Use lather from shampoo in place of shaving cream.

■ Leave a supply of personal products always packed in your bag.

■ On your travels, collect samples like shampoo and soap from hotel rooms and bring them home, even if not to your taste. Package them up in a small cosmetic bag (like the free ones from the cosmetic counter sales) and give them to a friend for a bon voyage gift. Alternately, keep them for visiting guests to your home or donate to a local shelter.

■ Leave your perfume bottle at home & take a travel atomizer ($6). Here's a tip: You can take a second atomizer & put vermouth in it for your martini's!

■ For the ultra organized, divide your personal care items by category and pack them inside plastic bags before you pack them in your toiletry kit. See page 77.

Packing Your Make Up Bag

■ Most importantly, never pack your make-up inside your toiletry kit. In case of leakage, you don't want it to ruin expensive makeup. Keep your make up in a separate zippered bag (I like one that's brightly colored so it's easy to locate in a black bag).

■ Place each item inside a small re-sealable plastic bag just in case something leaks.

■ Cut a piece of plastic the same size as your face powder container and place it in the top. This prevents the powder from spilling when you open it.

■ Small cosmetic bags with zippers make great places to keep costume jewelry, different currencies, and other small items.

■ Invest in one of the all-in-one cosmetic creams, the kind that serves as day moisturizer, night cream, and under eye cream. This eliminates the need to carry three different items.

■ Make up can take up a lot of room so ask at the cosmetic counter for a sample of foundation in the color that you usually use. This should last at least 5 days.

■ Use a combination shampoo/conditioner instead of taking two bottles.

■ Instead of taking a bottle of fingernail polish remover, which would create a disaster if spilled, pack pre-moistened polish remover pads.

■ Consider traveling with make-up remover towelettes. Easy to and can be used when water is not readily available.

Tips for Healthier Trips

■ Take a list of your medications with you.

■ Also, keep a list in your wallet of the medications that you can't take, i.e. the medicines you are allergic to.

■ Keep a Medic Alert card in your wallet or purse if you have a medical problem or allergies. It is also advisable to put your blood type on it.

■ Update any prescriptions and take extra with you. Be sure to keep all medicine in their original, labeled bottles to avoid problems.

■ Since a lot of prescriptions and vitamins come in large quantities, ask your pharmacist to give you the smallest bottle they have for your medications and have him print out a new label for it. That way you can take only what you need with you and save space at the same time.

■ Pack a small collapsible cup for taking medication.

■ Ask your doctor about traveling with Pepto Bismol® to ease upset stomach, nausea & diarrhea. Many travelers won't leave home without it.

■ If you have allergic reactions to certain foods, have someone write on a card, in the language of the countries that you are visiting, the foods you cannot eat.

■ For muscle relaxation, pack a few air-activated heat wraps in your bag. Just open the pouch and the single-use wrap begins to warm up when exposed to air.

■ Budget bottled water into your travel budget. Avoid possible problems by only drinking bottled water, especially in exotic areas where the hygiene is questionable. You can drink local water if it's been boiled (such as coffee & tea), and remember, even the ice in your drink may not have been made out of boiled water. It's worth the extra money. Bottled drinks, such as wine, beer and carbonated drinks are also usually safe.

■ Consider packing some refreezable ice cubes which safely chill drinks anywhere the water is "questionable."

■ Avoid fresh fruits and vegetables which might have been washed in contaminated water. Peeled fruit is usually safe.

■ Carry some pre-packaged peanut butter crackers on long trips. They provide protein and carbohydrates when you can't find a meal that suits your taste.

■ Remember to pack a pair of extra reading glasses or spare contacts. If glasses get damaged it may be difficult to replace them. In foreign countries it will be even more difficult.

■ Pack disposable travel-sized antibacterial wipes for a quick clean up before meals and after you've experienced a restroom on the road. Also great after touching escalator hand rails, elevator buttons, door knobs, etc.

"When in Rome,
do as the Romans do."

Anonymous

-10-
Laundry On The Go

I've discovered from polling my audiences over the years that it's about even: 50% of travelers do laundry along the road, and 50% don't. Half the world is of the mind that they are on vacation & they aren't doing laundry (or are on business and their company is paying for it). To them, it's worth the extra money (and extra clothes & luggage) to have someone do it for them. If you're one of those people, skip this chapter.

The other-half follow the philosophy of doing laundry along the way instead of using expensive hotel laundry services. By washing out a few items every other day, you can extend your travel wardrobe and pack lighter. This not only saves money but it saves valuable vacation time. Who wants to spend a day at the laundromat if you don't have to?

If you're still with me, here's what I do:

Home Made Laundry Kit

Pack the following items in a gallon size plastic bag:

❏ Braided Elastic Laundry Line

❏ Inflatable Hanger

❏ Sink Stopper

❏ Multi-Purpose Travel Soap

❏ Micro-fiber Travel Towel

❏ Stain Removal Stick

Braided Elastic Laundry Line means you don't have to pack clothes pins because the elastic holds the clothes securely.

Multi Purpose Travel Soap is not only great for clothes but can be used for your hands or as shampoo, or for washing up camp dishes. It works in cold water, hot water, salt water, etc. A traveler once told me he wears all his dirty clothes right into the shower & starts with his head: washes his hair, his clothes, body, down to his socks. (Most women are horrified at the thought of this but know men that would do it!). If you'll be using this in the outdoors, be certain to purchase one that is biodegradable.

A Sink Stopper to plug a drain. Many hotels do not provide these because they'd prefer you to send your laundry out to be cleaned. Travel with a multi-purpose, 5 inch diameter, thin, rubber disk. It's also useful for opening jars, removing lint from clothing and as a bath plug.

A Travel Towel made out of Micro Fiber. Micro Fiber absorbs water quickly. Roll up your washed items in it to absorb the water and your clothes will dry faster. I prefer the large size, you can also use it as a cover-up for your swimsuit, as a beach towel, wrap your hair in it so you don't have to pack a hairdryer and even use as a blanket on the plane in a pinch!

Inflatable Hangers made of durable vinyl inflate to allow your drip dry blouses, bathing suits, and sweaters to dry without hanger creases. Also provides you with extra hangers. They can be used also at home for fine lingerie. And you won't get rust from scary old hotel hangers on your nice clean clothes.

A Stain Removal Stick will save the day. Always keep one in your laundry kit for quick spot removal when you don't have time to wash.

A Zip Clean Travel Washing Machine really works! When it comes to doing laundry in the sink, do you ever wonder how clean the sink really is? Use a gallon size plastic bag with a zip top closure as a mini-washing machine (two gallon bag for larger items). Just put in your socks, soap, and water and agitate or knead it for awhile. Repeat with clean water for the "rinse-cycle". Pack pre-measured travel soap in snack sized bags and combine all your laundry items such as: laundry line, inflatable hangers, etc. inside a gallon size bag so you always have everything organized.

More Laundry Secrets

■ Some old style sinks are funneled too deep for the disc sink-stopper to work efficiently. For these you can use a small heavy children's rubber ball (2"). This stops up any size drain and you also have something to play with along your travels.

■ Ice cubes work great on a grease spill on clothing while dining out if nothing else is available. The stain won't set in.

■ Sample sizes of dishwashing liquid, mailed as promotions, are great for getting grease out of clothes, and they are packaged not to break.

■ Don't forget to take a small packet of cold water soap just in case you find hot water unavailable.

■ Take along a small a spray bottle and when you have a wrinkle in cottons, linen or any washable item, simply fill the bottle with tap water, spray the wrinkles; in a short time the wrinkles will disappear.

■ Use mesh laundry bags for packing similar items together making them easier to find. For example, underwear, t-shirts and especially small items like socks.

■ Compression bags work great for dirty laundry and especially for damp work out clothes that don't have time to dry before you pack them. See pages 27-28.

■ And be sure to pack some dryer sheets to use if you find a dryer on your travels.

■ Think twice about traveling in jeans. If you need to wash them, they'll take a very long time to dry.

"The journey,
not the arrival matters."

T.S. Eliot (1888-1965)

-11-
Tips for Plane Trips

There are many different forms of transportation, and plane travel can be one of the most stressful, if you're not prepared.

One of the most important tips is to be sure to arrive at the airport with plenty of time to get through security checkpoints, check your bags (if you're checking any) and still have some spare time for last minute things like making a phone call or using the facilities. Remember, it's recommended that you arrive at least 90 min. prior to domestic flights and 2 hours for International flights (check with your airline, I like to arrive even earlier).

To help ensure a smooth trip, it's important to plan ahead and have certain essentials with you to make the trip more enjoyable. The following suggestions will help you maximize your time in the airport & arrive rested & ready to hit the ground running after any flight.

Tips

■ If you have a cold or any other physical problem that you are concerned about, be sure to consult your physician before any flight.

■ At the ticket counter, always have the ticket agent confirm your return coupons, as well as reserve your seat if you don't already have one.

■ To minimize waits, opt for the first flight of the day.

■ Check your baggage claim tickets immediately when they are stapled into your ticket jacket and attached to your luggage. Make sure that they match and that you have all of them.

Everyone makes mistakes, and it's easier to catch them right away.

■ Before leaving home for the airport, always call to find out if your flight is on time. Do so likewise when picking someone up at the airport, for often weather conditions cause delays, and you shouldn't spend needless time (and money for parking) waiting for their arrival.

■ When picking someone up at the airport, arrange to meet them outside the departure area (the opposite of what you would normally do). There usually isn't a huge crush of cars all vying for the curb at the same time like there is in the arrivals.

■ Once you are at the airport, check the monitors to see if your flight is still on time.

■ Enjoy your time at the airport. Use it to check out the different shops, which include bookstores, card stores, and various specialty boutiques.

■ In large airports where you may have to change terminals to catch your next flight, inquire about a shuttle service before deplaning. This saves times and allows you to head directly to the service without waiting in endless lines.

■ If your checked luggage arrives damaged, report it as soon as possible to an airline representative before you leave the airport.

■ One of my favorite tips is: Fly the day before you need to be at your destination. This helps alleviate stress in case you encounter weather or mechanical delays along the way. Your best bet is to arrive at your destination rested and relaxed, so you can start your holiday immediately, or with a small amount of rest time.

Tips to Help Reduce Jet Lag

For many travelers, the real turbulence begins after a flight. Crossing time zones disrupts your body clock and can lead to sleepy days & sleepless nights, and more.

To help prevent jet lag, get plenty of sleep before your trip and drink water on the plane, not alcohol. The dry air in airplanes causes dehydration and drinking plenty of non-alcoholic fluids helps counter this. (However, when I told my father this tip, his reply was, "Why on earth would I fly if I can't have a drink?" As with all the tips in this book, some will work for you, some won't.)

A few other suggestions

■ Limit your intake of caffeine and salt, eat bland foods a few days before the trip, and don't eat spicy foods en route.

■ Adjust your sleeping habits before leaving home. Check the time zone to which you're headed and go to sleep an hour earlier than usual (or later, depending on which direction). Allow your body to adjust.

■ Once you're on the plane, change your watch to your destination time zone. I don't know if it's all psychological, but it works for me.

■ And, upon arrival, take a long warm shower. More than a few travelers have suggested this tip. They say it helps restore some hydration to your body (and it helps wake you up).

Food In the Air

■ Isn't it funny, for years we all joked about airline food and now we miss it. Call your airline to see if there will be a meal offered (and whether it's complimentary) and ask if you can order a special meal in advance. Hey, stranger things have happened.

■ Always travel with food. Ramen noodles and instant soup can be mixed with a cup of hot water to make an instant meal on the plane. Dried cranberries, nuts & nutrition bars are also good.

■ Bring some extra food or breakfast bars for the outer pocket of your carry on just in case you become stranded in an airport. Sometimes the airport closes down early.

Comfort En Route

■ Travel with your own Plane Pocket of Comfort, which includes a blanket, eye shades, inflatable pillow & ear plugs all packed in one bag. See page 76.

■ An inflatable neck pillow is perfect to save your neck from kinks & a lumbar pillow used at the small of your back greatly relieves tired shoulders. I always travel with my own neck & lumbar pillow in my carry-on bag.

■ Here's a unique plane pillow idea: Bring an inflatable beach ball. When you get on the plane and are ready for a head rest, blow the ball half way up or until comfortable. You can have fun with it when you get off the plane.

■ Sleeping is easier when you block out light & sound. Pack eye-shades and ear-plugs for uninterrupted sleep while flying.

■ On long flights (especially international flights) wear casual clothing and then change in the airport restroom before claiming your baggage. The key here is to be comfortable.

■ Pack a pair of socks in your carry-on (in case you're not wearing any). Keeps your toes warm.

■ After your flight reaches cruising altitude, remove your shoes and scrunch your toes around — it helps!

■ To help circulation, prop your feet on your carry-on bag. (Of course make sure that you don't have any breakables near the surface).

■ For contact wearers: Carry a travel-sized bottle of saline solution in your carry-on. The air on planes & air conditioning can dry them out at high elevations. Be sure to bring your spare glasses and a lens case with you in your carry-on. You don't want to be without these items in the event that your checked luggage is lost.

■ Keep a small spray bottle of water in your carry-on to keep your face and arms moisturized at high elevations. Also a travel-sized bottle of lotion and eye drops.

■ The best solution many have found to keep ears clear while flying is to chew gum. Use it on both the ascent and descent. Or try a sip of water from your water bottle. It helps you stay hydrated in a dry environment as well.

■ Many travelers recommend EarPlanes™, a product made specifically to relieve ear pressure when you take off and land.

Airplane Seating

■ Couples may wish to occupy facing seats on the aisle to [1] avoid climbing over passengers on the way to the rest room, [2] there is a higher probability of having a vacant seat since the center seat is usually always the last one assigned, and [3] you are guaranteed the use of at least one arm rest.

■ Request an emergency exit row for more leg room. Be sure you are capable of assisting in an emergency and fit the criteria for this row.

■ A window seat is best for sleeping. No one will crawl over you to get to the restroom or the overhead compartment.

■ An aisle seat is best for stretching your legs and for those who may need to use the facilities often.

■ Request a bulkhead seat if you are traveling with children, or a wheelchair or cane. (Keep in mind that you may be sitting beside people with special needs and may be interrupted often.)

■ Ask the flight attendant if the plane is fully booked. If not, you may be able to make yourself more comfortable by moving to another area of the plane to stretch out.

More Tips for Plane Trips

■ Take your seat immediately when they begin to start boarding your row on the plane. This way you are almost guaranteed your seat in case of over-booking, as you will already be sitting in it.

■ Always leave your shoes on until the aircraft has reached cruising altitude- just in case you have to evacuate the aircraft in an emergency.

■ If you like to read on planes, bring a book light. Sometimes the plane light at your seat might not be working. Or use your travel flashlight that you have packed for emergencies.

-12-
Car Tips for Road Trips

Whether you're packing a car, a mini-van or an RV, there are a few basic principles to keep in mind. #1) Keep the front seat area as the command center — no distractions. #2) When packing the car, place the heaviest items on the bottom and don't pack higher than the seat back in order to keep items from shifting in a suddden stop. #3) Pack the most important items that you'll need on your trip last, so they're the easiest to find!

Front Seat Area

■ Keep your cell phone in the front seat area and use a hands free adapter for safety. Better yet, have someone traveling with you make the call.

■ Keep your travel atlas with-in easy reach: In the pocket of the door.

■ Instead of struggling with a huge a map, cut out the area you'll be traveling through, use a highlighter to outline the route and place it inside a plastic sleeve for quick reference.

■ Pack your car's emergency kit and first aid kit under your seats for easy access.

■ Clean out your glove compartment and put only what you need back in. Keep a flashlight handy for emergencies or just to read a map. Also keep tissues, wet-ones & sunglasses close at hand.

■ Keep a compass in your glove compartment for finding your way in unfamiliar areas. This has saved many marriages.

Middle Seats

■ A backseat organizer is perfect for keeping items from rolling around the floor of your car. These hook over the headrest and have multiple pockets for such items as: umbrellas, magazines, paper towels, water bottles, etc. You can pack one for kids with snacks and make it an activity center filled with things to do while in the car.

■ Use every bit of space: A 12 pack of soda/beverages fits under the middle seat of a van.

■ Freeze a few water bottles before you leave home. That way you have very cold water to drink as it starts melting. Better to freeze only half the bottle — the water may expand sufficiently to cause unnoticed cracks in the bottle — unnoticed until the ice melts that is. Also, if you only freeze half the bottle, you won't have to wait 3 hours to get the first few sips out.

Rear Section of Car

■ If your car has a lift-up compartment in the back like a tire-well it's perfect for packing: breakables, gifts, items that might get crushed (like a bottle of wine). Line it first with a blanket.

■ Always conceal valuables in your trunk or under cover for protection.

■ Pack the heaviest items in your car first, on the bottom, & then pack the perimeter with soft, squishable items that won't break and will help to cushion the items packed in middle.

■ The cardboard six packs that markets handout for multiple wine purchases are very helpful. They fold flat when not in use and, when needed, keep new purchases from rolling around in boxes & totes.

■ Collapsible crates (available for about $5 at home improvement stores) are great for car travel. Open and stack when needed, collapse & save space when you don't.

■ Pack a different colored bag per person. Brightly colored tote bags help identify what's organized where. Squish, stuff & stack.

■ Pack coolers on the bottom & stack items around them. Do not pack coolers in the center as they are too hard to reach and drag out of the center.

■ Pack all your sun/beach items together in one tote bag: Sunscreen, sunglasses, swimsuit, hat, towel, etc. so you can hit the beach running.

Car Tips for Kid Trips

■ Place an upside down cardboard box between the kids in the middle or backseat. This will serve two purposes: Act as a writing surface, and also keep them separated.

■ Keep an empty baby wipes container (the square, pop-up kind) filled with used plastic grocery sacks in your car. On trips, long or short, you always have a bag handy for trash, to put dirty kids clothes, or wet swim items in. Keep it under the seat.

■ Office supply stores have a great variety of plastic containers that teenagers really like. Packed with some fun gel pens, paper & notepads, this makes a nice gift to give them before you go and keeps them busy en route.

■ Keep a backpack fully stocked within arms reach for each child.

■ Use cookie sheets as drawing surfaces for your children. Cut a piece of non skid shelf liner to fit the inside and use the ones with the lip on the edge to help keep pens from sliding off. You can find used ones at thrift stores or garage sales.

■ Before you spend money at a specially store, check out your kitchen: A 9"x13" covered tin cake pan makes a great "lap desk" for kids in the car. Pack all their colored pencils, paper, crafts inside and they have a flat surface to write on the top. Cover a cookie sheet with non-skid shelf liner and you have a surface that toys that won't slide off of.

- Pack pillows & blankets for everyone (& you'll have an extra blanket when you get there).

- Here's an easy solution to the age-old question of who gets the front seat, window, etc. (if you have children who are born on odd/even days). On odd numbered days, the child with the odd numbered birthday would have the first choice and on the even numbered day, etc.

- A blank map of the US per child can be colored as a tag/license plate from that state is spotted.

- Pack a jump rope in your backseat organizer so you're ready to burn off some energy when you reach the rest area.

- A Frisbee is a must for car travel with kids. They are inexpensive, fun to play with at rest stops and can be used as plates in a pinch.

- Keep a pair of flip flops (thongs) for each child in the back seat pocket for quick rest stops so they don't have to put their shoes on.

- Plan your picnics at playgrounds so there's something fun & new for the kids to do while you relax and have something to eat.

- Pack a mesh drawstring bag for wet jackets, clothing or towels. The open mesh allows the air to circulate so you won't end up with mildew on your items.

- Keep some extra kitchen towels in the car for use when your coffee spills or to catch crumbs when eating in the car. With a splash of water you can do a quick clean up also.

- Pack lots of garbage bags for all types of uses.

-13-
Cruising Tips

Cruising is one of the most popular vacation choices offered to travelers. Although cruises have been around for years, there are now many more lines and itineraries to choose from. These days, it seems like everyone is cruising.

The benefit of a cruise holiday is that almost every detail of your trip is taken care of for you. As most cruises are sold exclusively through travel agents, once you have decided which one is for you, you can relax and leave the planning to them.

Be familiar with your cruise line's brochure and know exactly what is and what is not included in the price. This varies greatly from line to line. For example, some cruise lines include your shore excursions in the total cruise fare, while most do not, and this can make a huge difference in price if you intend to take advantage of the ship's tour program. There are also some wonderful lecture programs available on some Cruise lines which really enhances your experience on board. Be sure to check in advance.

Luggage tips

What's one of the best things about cruising? You only have to unpack once! However, since you don't have to lug your stuff around for 2 weeks, travelers tend to pack more for cruise vacations. Hopefully the following tips will help you pack less & more efficiently for your cruise.

While the majority of cruise lines do not have specific baggage allowances, you have to consider how you're getting to the port. If you're driving to the port, there's no problem. However, airlines do have baggage allowances, so it is recommended that you check with the airline on which you're traveling to see what those allowances are. And, keep in mind that once at your destination, transfer vehicles may have baggage restrictions.

Remember that checked baggage might not be accessible at all times. A solution to this problem is: a 16" rolling tote bag. This bag plus a small tote bag allows you to carry on everything you'd need for the first 1-2 days of your cruise, including a change of clothes for the first evening upon embarkation. The wheels make it a breeze to carry heavy items such as medicines, cameras, binoculars, etc. up gangways and through long cruise ship terminals. See page 36 for more information on the 16" rolling tote bag.

Tips

- Remember to bring your travel and health insurance information with you and have it handy at all times.

- Double check that your identification and travel tickets are in your personal carry-on bag and available at all times.

- As with any type of travel, never pack anything of value in your checked luggage.

- When you pack your cruise carry-on, try packing everything you will need for the first three days in this bag. With the chance of lost or delayed luggage, especially if you arrive at your destination the same day you set sail, you may sail without your checked bags.

- In addition to a 16" rolling tote & a small tote bag, most cruisers should be able to pack enough clothing into a 24" rolling suitcase for a 1-2 week cruise (See Cruise Wardrobe Planner page 105). Remember, there will be times when you will need to handle your luggage on your own and you want to be able to stack and roll easily. Consider expandable luggage because you just know you're going to do some shopping.

- Always be sure to place an ID tag on your bag. Most cruise lines will give you special baggage tags with your cruise documentation and instructions on how, when & where to place them on your bags before you leave home.

■ If you are traveling a great distance to the port of departure, it is highly recommended that you arrive at least one day in advance of your sailing date. This will give your checked luggage a chance to catch up to you if it is delayed, since most travel packages are scheduled to get you to the port just before sailing. This also allows you to begin your holiday a bit more rested and relaxed and allows you to explore the port city if you wish to. While this would most probably be at an additional expense to you, ask your travel agent about the pre- and post-cruise packages that most cruise lines offer, usually at a terrific savings.

■ Another option for your luggage is to forward it to the ship before your cruise or forward it home after the cruise. To do this, simply contact the shipping company recommended by the cruise line on which you're traveling.

Organizing Your Cruise Wardrobe

The right clothing can make a big difference in the enjoyment of your cruise. First and foremost, dress for comfort. Daily life aboard ship and in ports of call is laid-back and casual. Wear whatever makes you feel most comfortable-sportswear, shorts, sundresses, slacks, and so on. Warmer climates call for clothing made of lightweight, breathable fabrics. For cooler climates pack casual clothes that can be layered easily and possibly a raincoat and waterproof hat or umbrella and gloves.

Don't forget your swimsuit — most cruise ships have pools and whirlpools. You may wish to bring more than one swimsuit for the water, if you'll be spending much time in and around it. Remember to wear shoes and a cover-up over your bathing suit when walking through the interior of the ship. If you'd like to jog on deck or work out in the fitness center, bring workout gear.

Footwear should include comfortable walking shoes for visits ashore and sandals or rubber-soled shoes for strolling on deck.

Dress

Evening dress usually falls into three categories Casual, Informal & Formal. Each night a daily program will be delivered to your cabin announcing the suggested dress for the following evening.

Casual

Casual means exactly what it says, comfortable relaxed clothing. But not sweat suits or shorts. Some cruise lines allow jeans in the dining room for dinner, but not all. Check with your travel agent or refer to your cruise brochure/documents.

Informal

During informal nights, dresses or pantsuits for women and jackets (tie optional) for men are standard.

Formal

On formal evenings, women usually wear cocktail dresses or palazzo pants with a dressy top and men a business suit or tuxedo. A jacket and tie is also acceptable for men.

There are approximately two formal nights per week.

Ask your travel agent to find out specifically how many casual, informal, and formal nights your cruise will have. This varies from line to line and itinerary. Make a list of each and what clothes you plan to wear. This cuts down on over-packing.

Also ask your travel agent for suggestions if you need additional advice or ask him/her to refer you to a client that has just returned from the cruise line you are sailing on. First hand knowledge is invaluable.

Use the Cruise Wardrobe Planner on the following page to help you organize your wardrobe.

Pack It Up—Cruise Wardrobe Planner

	Port	Daytime Outfit	Evening Outfit	*	Special Events & Activities
Day 1					
Day 2					
Day 3					
Day 4					
Day 5					
Day 6					
Day 7					

*Use this column to indicate ship's suggested evening dress C- Casual   I-Informal   F-Formal

©Pack It Up

Wardrobe Planning Tips

■ Most importantly, take into consideration the type of cruising that you will be doing. Obviously, a weekend cruise is more casual than a world cruise.

■ Remember that black is always formal (and dark blue as well). You can dress-up an outfit many different ways with just a minimal amount of accessories when you wear black, and save purchasing additional clothes.

■ Many people choose cruising as a holiday because they enjoy "dressing" for dinner and having the opportunity to wear fine jewelry. This seems to work well for most people, but remember that you must get to the ship via airplanes, buses, etc., and that jewelry should be kept in a safe when you're not wearing it. This can be very time consuming and worrisome, so it is suggested that you carefully weigh the pros and cons of bringing valuables on your cruise.

■ Many cruises offer "Theme Nights" and your travel agent will supply you with a list of those in advance. Ask your friends and relatives if they have an item of clothing that you can borrow before you purchase something that you probably won't wear again in the near future.

■ The potential expense of a cruise wardrobe is the formal attire. Women passengers wear almost anything from nice pants to exquisite sequin gowns. Unless a gentleman enjoys wearing a tuxedo, it's not necessary to bring one. A dark suit with tie works fine. Usually the longer the cruise the fancier the dress is, but even that rule of thumb is variable.

■ For formal night, a woman would feel quite acceptable in a medium-to-long dress, or a skirt with a fancy top/blouse. A black skirt works well, as you can change many different tops and belts to dress it up or down. As well, a pair of fancy black pants with silk/polyester blouses and low black heels can turn simpler clothes into a variety of looks.

■ Longer faux pearl necklaces can be more versatile and shortened with a pearl clip for a different look. Matching earrings with a bit of rhinestone look very elegant.

■ Rhinestone necklaces and bracelets are fun to wear but expensive to buy. Ask someone who just returned from a cruise if they might have some you could borrow, or check second-hand stores for a great savings.

■ Don't forget an evening clutch bag or one with a strap. Again, stay with a basic color scheme and check department or vintage clothing store for specials. A money saving tip: convert your simple black travel purse to a fancy evening bag by simply pinning a rhinestone pin to the outside. It really dresses it up! Tuck the straps to the inside of the bag and you have a nice clutch.

■ Pack your jewelry inside your evening bag so you always know where it is. Do not pack valuable jewelry.

■ If you are on a clothing budget, ask friends and family to lend you some fancy things they may have just sitting around the house. And check into formal wear rentals for women as well as men.

■ Elastic waisted clothing is essential for those who enjoy eating (and isn't that one of the main attractions of a cruise)? Here's a tip: Use a heavy duty rubber band if your pants are too tight and loop it through the button & buttonhole. It's said that the salt air shrinks your clothes when you're at sea; either way, be comfortable.

General Cruising Tips

■ Pack an outfit that can double as exercise wear. Many passengers discover great programs onboard designed for all levels of fitness for example, a walk-a-mile class and wish they had brought something to exercise in. It's a great way to meet friends and also justify that second helping of cherries jubilee.

■ If you are a serious exercise enthusiast, check into different cruise lines. Most offer fantastic exercise programs and state of-the-art gym equipment. On some lines, entire theme cruises are planned around the exercise program. Be sure to confirm that the ship you choose has a fitness director onboard. Some ships even have incentive programs in which you are awarded gifts for your participation.

■ Ships' activities are a great way to meet new friends. All lines' activities vary, so ask your travel agent if he/she has a recent copy of the daily activities program from the ship you are looking into. Arts and crafts classes & solo-travelers get together are just a few activities that are often offered.

■ Bring a bathing cap (which can double as a shower cap in a pinch!). Many cruise ship swimming pools are salt water, which can be damaging to your hair if it's chemically treated or very dry. Take extra conditioner along for your hair just in case.

■ A pashmina (wrap) is a must if you tend to chill easily. Whether for a nice stroll out on deck under the stars or for the air-conditioning in the lounges, you'll be glad that you brought it. Black is a good color choice as it can be used on formal nights as well (and won't show dirt as easily as white).

■ A pareo makes a handy cover-up for the pool or beach. It's easy to tie and wear while sitting at the counter for a refreshing drink, or to throw over you when you've had too much sun. Please see page 121 for ideas on how to tie your Pareo.

■ A packable straw hat is perfect for a cruise, rolls to pack and won't fray or crack.

■ You should always pack comfortable shoes when traveling but this hold true especially on a ship that is constantly moving. Comfortable walking shoes for visits ashore and sandals or rubber soled shoes for strolling on deck. Low heels are much more practical for evening wear

■ If you are traveling with children or grandchildren, make sure that the ship you are on encourages them. There are certain lines that specialize in children's programs with entire daily schedules printed just for them. Generally, the peak cruising times for children are major holidays, so if you prefer the company of adults only, heed this last information and choose your schedule accordingly.

■ As the sun's rays are much stronger at sea than on land due to the lack of pollution and clouds screening out the sun's harmful rays, wear extra sunscreen and a head covering if you are susceptible to burns. A visor is helpful if you like to read in the sun, and don't forget the effects of sun reflected off water if you are poolside or at the beach. The same effect exists with snow on the colder itineraries such as Alaska and Scandinavia. And don't overlook protection for your lips! Select a lip balm that includes a sunscreen to help combat the effects of all the wind, sun and salt air.

■ Throw in the book that you haven't had time to read yet. Most ships have excellent libraries, but on the chance that yours doesn't, take it along. A tip on ships' libraries: check out the book selection as soon as you have a chance. Passengers tend to linger over books that they've borrowed, and the selection is greatly reduced after the first few days at sea.

■ Instead of packing your old paperback to take home, suggest a paperback exchange, if there isn't one already setup by the staff. This is a great way to meet someone and trade your old book for a new one for the trip home.

■ If you do forget something, remember that the ship's boutique usually has any item that you may need. In addition, check their daily specials, as many a great buy has been made when you take into account that the majority of these shops are duty-free. Even on cruises with ideal shopping destinations, remember that the ship's boutiques have competitive prices.

■ If you wear pantyhose, bring a few pairs with you. This is one article of clothing that varies greatly from one brand to another, especially the size.

■ Give yourself permission to take a night off and just relax! Why not use the time to do some laundry while you're finishing up that book you've been too busy to read? Most large cruise ships have laundry rooms with coin operated washers & dryers and even some with irons and ironing boards. This works especially well for 10 day or longer cruises as you don't have to pack as many clothes.

■ Take a postcard of your ship with you ashore. This way you have a picture to show drivers, etc. where you need to return in case there's a language barrier.

Communication At Sea

Direct ship-to-shore telephones are provided in most guest staterooms on most ships. Check with your Travel Agent or cruise brochure.

Many cruise lines provide "communications cards" when you book your cruise or receive your tickets. Distribute these to friends and relatives so they will know how to contact you in case of an emergency back home or just so say hello.

On most cruise ship guests can send and receive electronic mail in real-time, via a high speed satellite link 24 hours a day, satellite conditions permitting.

The ship usually prints a capsule of the day's news happening around the world. Check the ships library to see if any newspapers were brought aboard in port.

Each day you will receive a log of the daily activities that will take place with the time and location listed. It is a good idea to read this every evening so you don't miss out on any activities that may interest you. If you're not sure of your way around the ship, and did not receive a map upon embarkation, ask the front office for one to assist you in getting around.

Money Matters

The majority of all cruise lines have a "Sign-As-You-Sail" policy for all purchases made onboard. You simply sign your name and cabin or account number, and show your ship's account card, which doubles as a boarding pass in some instances. You may choose to add a gratuity on the bottom of the chit, if it has not been added automatically.

For ease in settling your account, most cruise lines encourage you to leave an imprint of your credit card with the front office during the first few days of the cruise. Your itemized bill will be sent to your cabin directly, usually the day before you disembark for approval and inspection. This eliminates standing in line on the last day.

Selecting a Cabin

Your travel agent is the most important wealth of knowledge for all your travel needs. But you must provide some information about yourself so he/she can find the cabin best suited to your needs. Here are some suggestions:

- If you tend to get seasick or think you might, a mid-ships cabin would be a good idea. Away from the pitching and rolling of the topside and lower decks, you will be the most stable.

- Do you want/need a TV, a suite or verandah? Check the prices in the different categories. Do you need a porthole? If you don't plan on spending much time in your cabin, a porthole is an added expense that you may not need.

- Are you a light sleeper? Check where the lounges are located, as a late-night band might keep you awake.

- If you prefer a queen or king size bed, make sure that the ship you have chosen can accommodate your request. Some of the older ships are furnished with only twin beds.

- If you use a wheelchair, make sure that your cabin and bathroom are accessible. And make sure there is an elevator in the vicinity.

Read the diagram in the brochure to find out about the layout of the ship and ask your travel agent's advice, too.

Dining Tips

■ Most cruise ships offer you the choice of two sittings generally called early and late. The early sitting usually begins at 6 p.m. and the late around 8 p.m. As usually your evenings' entertainment follows your dinner, second sitting is generally for the younger or more late-night sort of person who enjoys a show beginning usually after 10 p.m. The first sitting show usually begins around 8 p.m.

■ If you do have a preference in sittings, be sure to request it from your travel agent. Remember, though, that while the line will try to accommodate your request, it may not always be possible to do so.

■ Also, request to sit with any specific friends you are traveling with. Table sizes run anywhere from an intimate table for two to a large table of eight. Many passengers prefer a large table, using the philosophy that out of eight people chances are there will be some that are interesting conversationalists.

■ If you have received your seating arrangements and they are not what you requested, contact the Maitre d' as soon as possible (or the person in charge of the sitting assignments). For some passengers, this is the most important part of their cruise. Remember, a smile and a polite handshake go a long distance to remedy a situation.

■ If you have special dietary requirements, request these when you are booking your cruise. Make sure that the ship you're cruising on can accommodate your requirements. Remember that this is an extra service, so patience and understanding go a long way during the first few meals with a new waiter.

Seasickness

With today's modern technology and stabilizers, there is little chance of seasickness among passengers. But, if you are susceptible to motion sickness, be sure to check with your physician before leaving home. There are many different products on the market to help, though these may have different side effects for different people.

■ Motion Bands, a non-medicinal cure for seasickness (and most motion sickness), is a favorite among many passengers. Elasticized wrist bands that apply slight pressure on the acupressure point near each wrist that controls nausea.

■ For severe cases of seasickness, there is an injection available on most ships from the physician. Consult the hospital staff at home and onboard before making any decisions.

■ A few suggestions to help queasy stomachs: Dry foods, such as bread, breadsticks, or crackers, help to settle the uneasy feeling experienced in rough seas. Also suggested is limiting intake of liquids.

Tips on Tipping

Tipping varies greatly from ship to ship for which service was performed and how. Some cruise lines have a "No tipping required" policy; however, most passengers choose to extend gratuities for a job well done. Some cruise lines automatically add tips on for certain services on board including bar service & even your cabin steward & waiter. Be sure to check.

Generally, you will receive with your documents an updated guideline regarding who, when, and how much you should tip, so you know ahead of time how much money to take with you, and if in doubt, ask once you are onboard. Following is a general guideline based on per person per day of your cruise:

Tipping Chart for Cruises	
Cabin steward	$3 per person per day
Asst. steward	$1.75 per person per day
Dining room waiter	$3 per person per day
Asst. waiter	$2 per person per day
Bus-help	$1 per person per day

Also, tipping of the Maitre d' and the head waiter for any special meals or assistance is customary $10-$20 at the end of the cruise. Tipping for wine stewards is recommended at 15-20 percent. A note: If you receive a complimentary bottle of wine, it is customary to tip the wine steward for this service as if you had purchased the wine yourself.

When to tip? The majority of passengers wait until the last evening of the cruise and personally thank the person for making their cruise so memorable. Envelopes are usually provided at the front office for your convenience.

More Tips

■ At the end of the cruise, usually the second to the last day, a disembarkation talk for all passengers is held. It is highly suggested that one member of each party or family attends because information is given regarding disembarkation procedures, customs, luggage tags, airline connections and so on. This will insure that you will have a pleasant, stress-free ending to your cruise.

■ On the last night of your cruise, you will need to place your luggage, with the provided luggage tags, outside your cabin before you retire. You will find ship specific information on board.

■ Place a card with your name and address inside your luggage, as well as on the outside.

■ Be sure to keep together your personal identification, airline tickets, customs forms, medications, and other important items along with the clothes and shoes you intend to wear the next day, during your trip home. Place them in your carry-on bag or on your person so you can access them easily.

"Never a ship sails out of the bay,
but carries my heart
as a stowaway."

Roselle Mercier Montgomery
(d. 1933)

-14-
Travel Scarf Tying

A scarf is the most versatile accessory in your travel wardrobe. It can redefine any look and create styles that are casual or formal, professional or adventurous.

By including the following scarves in your travels and using this chapter as your guide, you will learn how to extend your wardrobe without using valuable luggage space. You will also add glamour to your wardrobe without spending a lot of money.

These are three scarves that you should not leave home without. The style, size and method of tying is the real secret.

Oblong	10" x 54"
Square	34" x 34
Pareo	46" x 60"

Scarf Tips

■ Pack scarves in plastic bags to keep wrinkles to a minimum.

■ Silk scarves and natural fabrics are warmer than synthetics. Tuck them around the neck of a sweater to keep warm.

■ Scarves make great gifts. They pack flat and don't break.

■ The quality of scarves can vary greatly. Look for scarf edges that are rolled and stitched by hand, usually indicating a higher quality of scarf than those stitched by machine.

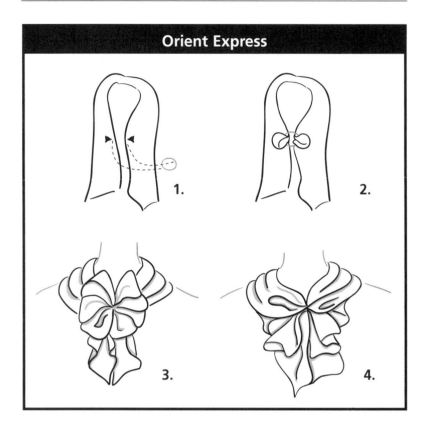

1. Drape oblong scarf around your neck.

2. Pinch only the inside edges of scarf at mid-way point.

3. Using a small covered elastic band, pull the edges slowly through until it forms a bow.

4. For another, more tailored look, place the elastic band in the back and pull the edges through towards you (the bow will be hidden).

As the name implies, this is a fast and elegant enhancement to any outfit. Works well with either silk or synthetic fabric. A small covered elastic band weighs less than a scarf-clip and usually works better (and less to pack!).

English Accent

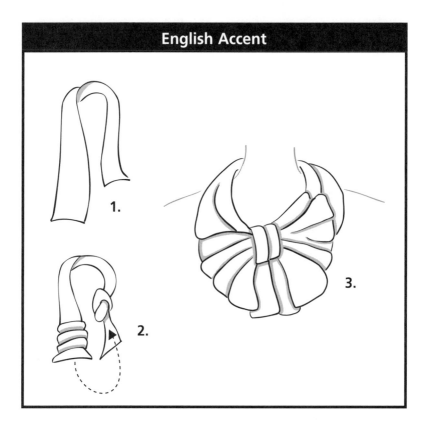

1. Place oblong scarf around neck keeping one end shorter than the other.

2. Tie a loose knot in the short end and fan pleat the long end until it's even with the short end. Hold pleats together and push up half-way through the knot.

3. Tighten the knot and fan as desired.

This works well with light synthetic fabrics. Worn with basic black or navy its perfect worn with a sweater, dress or jacket.

Segovian Secret

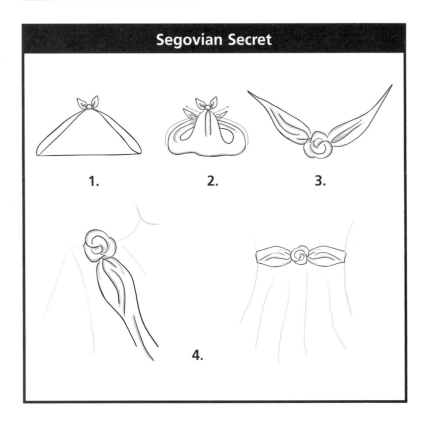

1.

2.

3.

4.

1. Fold square scarf into triangle and tie a small knot in top corner.

2. Take opposite ends and cross beneath the small knot, exchange hands.

3. Holding the ends, gently let the weight of the knot slowly slide down until the rose is formed.

4. Drape over shoulder for dramatic effect or around neck, waist or brim of a hat.

This works best with a silk scarf. Try a few different scarves to see varying results. Use a small safety pin to secure "rose" to garment.

English Accent

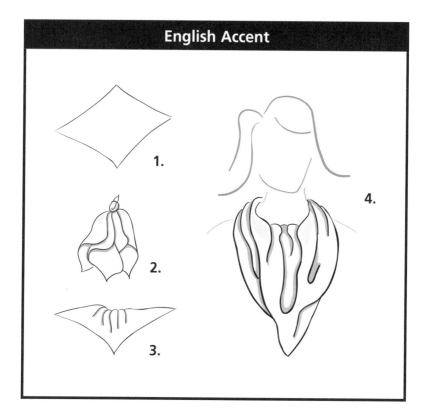

1. Place square scarf on a flat surface, wrong side up.

2. Tie a small knot at the center.

3. Fold scarf into a triangle with the knot on the inside.

4. Place the triangle in the front of the neck & tie at the back of the neck, arrange drape as desired.

This can be used as a substitute blouse under a V-neck sweater, cardigan or blazer. Perfect when traveling and laundry facilities are no where in sight!

St. Tropez Nights

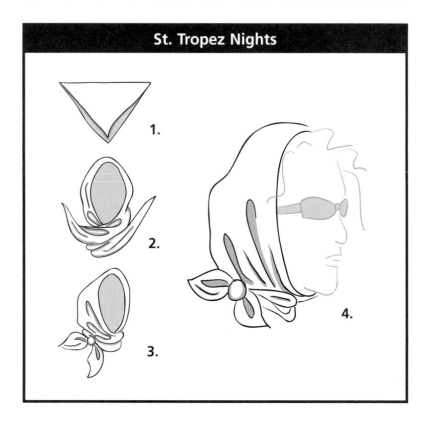

1. Fold a square scarf into a triangle.

2. Drape over head and cross the ends under chin.

3. Bring ends around to the back of neck & tie.

4. Arrange to frame face.

A touch of glamour, works well with any type of fabric. Good for a walk on a chilly evening or as a head covering for places of worship.

Patagonia Cover

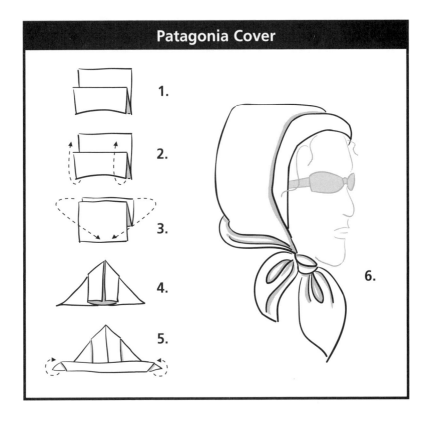

1. Place square scarf right side up on a flat surface. Fold the bottom edge to the top and then back down in half.

2. Taking bottom corners, turn scarf over, away from you.

3. Fold top two corners down to the center so they meet at the bottom edge.

4. Scarf will appear as shown.

5. From bottom, tightly roll the scarf until opening appears underneath.

6. Drape on head and tie under chin. Fold back edge framing face.

Works well with any type of fabrics. For warmth in very cold weather, use wool scarf instead of packing a wool hat. Saves space and your hairstyle.

North Cape

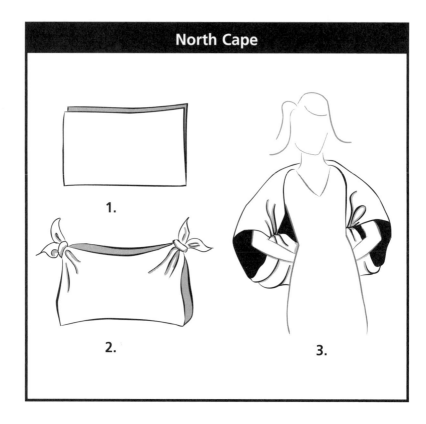

1. Fold pareo right sides together into a rectangle.

2. Tie the two corners together on each end.

3. Turn the pareo right side out and place your arms through the openings, keeping the knots under your arms.

This is great for taking cover from the hot sun or keeping warm in air-conditioned restaurants. For a more formal look, use a fancier pareo or make one by simply cutting any type of fabric and finishing the edges. (An interesting outing in a foreign country is to a fabric store. Thai silk works beautifully.)

Tahitian Pareo

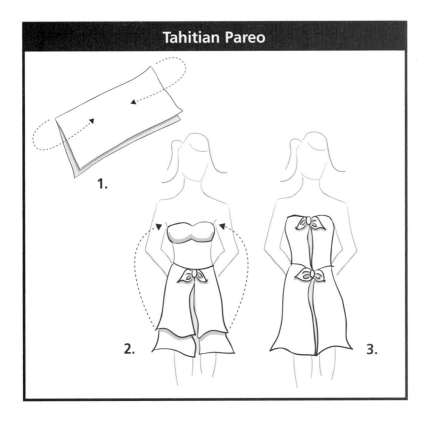

1. Fold pareo in half *right* sides together.

2. Place fold at waist and knot.

3. Take top layer from bottom edge and knot under your arm.

You can adjust the opening to the side for another look. Always travel with a pareo to use as a cover-up, beach towel or as a light blanket in a pinch.

"There are two kinds of travel —
first class and with children."

Robert Benchley
(1889-1945)

-15-
Great Ideas!

Over the years, I have picked up numerous travel and packing tips from the travelers that I have met along my journeys. From solo travelers to cruise passengers to tour members, they've passed on the following hints and swear to their effectiveness in making their trip just a little bit easier. Even the most seasoned traveler should be able to pick up a few new travel tips from among these:

■ Tip for golfers: Buy a cheap hockey stick and saw off the blade. Cut the remaining shaft to 46' (make sure the length is approx. 1" longer than your driver or 3 wood) Insert in golf bag. If your bag is dropped by the airlines the hockey stick will take the force of the drop and you will not have a bent or broken shaft.

■ For those travelers who enjoy making things with their hands, crocheting is a great way to kill time in airports, on long flights, train and bus rides. Take a crochet hook along and using locally bought yarn along the way, create something that will remind you of your trip once you get home.

■ Everyone knows it's a good idea to start your trip with new batteries for all your battery operated items. But here's a tip: Leave the new batteries in but reverse one so that the batteries are where they belong but they won't be dead when needed.

■ Here's a great tip for those who like to travel extremely light. When you arrive in a new country go to a backpacker's hostel and see who is ready to get rid of some gear...and buy it used. Conversely, when you're ready to leave, do the same.

■ When traveling over the holidays, ship your gifts in advance. No need to worry about delayed luggage and missing presents.

■ To secure your buttons, put a drop of Fray Check on each button prior to departure (available at fabric stores). It seals your buttons.

■ Pack travel binoculars (or a monocular) for walking tours, concerts, wildlife, etc. These fit into your pocket and most come with a case which includes a loop to attach on your belt.

■ A lot of travelers enjoy a drink before dinner or a nightcap, but room service can be expensive (or non existent at some destinations). Buy an 8oz (or 16 oz!) plastic bottle and fill with your favorite drink (vodka, gin, bourbon). Pack inside a plastic bag & slip inside your shoes in your checked-in luggage.

■ Wrap duct tape around a mailing tube. This will serve three purposes; it reinforces the tube, provides you with a lot of duct tape if you need it and you'll have a tube for bringing home any new art you purchase along the way.

■ Another use for duct tape while traveling: If the curtains of a hotel don't quite close all the way, tape them shut.

■ For safety when sightseeing: Wear a waist pack positioned in the front so when you stop to take photos, you don't have to set your purse on the ground. Your camera & film is easily accessible as well.

■ A very useful travel essential is a 3 foot retractable corded cable with a combination lock. It allows you to lock a group of luggage together when you go into a restaurant or secure your bags to the metal rack in a train compartment. It can also be used as a bike lock, ski lock, etc. Approx. $15

■ Since some socks can take forever to dry, try traveling with a pair or two of hiking sock liners. These not only help prevent blisters but drip dry quickly.

■ Take an emergency blanket and a $1 rain poncho. They both work great as a ground cover for a picnic, table cloth, luggage cover, coat, etc.

■ Can't seem to save enough money for your dream vacation? Make a "dream jar" by decorating a coffee can (or any container) with magazine photos of your dream destination. Put it in the kitchen and every time you decide to eat in instead of dining out, put the extra money you've saved into your "dream" vacation fund.

■ Save clean napkins from the breakfast table for your day's journey. They can provide a quick clean up.

■ Develop at least one roll of film before your vacation to ensure that your camera is still functioning. This is important for both new and old cameras alike.

■ Check batteries in your travel flashlight and remove them when not in use. For emergencies, place the flashlight near your bed when going to sleep.

■ Don't forget to take extra batteries for everything. They may be impossible to find, and also expensive, in certain countries. You don't want to waste precious sightseeing time in a frustrating search. This includes hearing aid batteries.

■ Always travel with safety pins. If a button pops off, use a safety pin.

■ Pack a small, foam-gripped pen on an 18 inch retractable cord that clips to your belt loop, or bag strap. It is small and conveniently accessible.

■ Another use for a hotel shower cap: It works great for keeping your saddle dry on your bike from rain and dew. The elastic fits snuggly around it and won't blow off from the wind.

■ If you enjoy visiting wineries on your travels, pack a corkscrew. Sampling your new discoveries in your hotel room that night can be elegant — if you are prepared.

■ Dryer sheets or air freshners can be very useful while traveling: Freshen up a hotel room, drawer, closet, rental car, shoes, etc.

Great Ideas For Empty 35 MM Film Canisters

■ Save 35mm film canisters to store small amounts of lotions, liquid detergent, hair gel, etc. when traveling. They are small, and the caps hold liquids without spilling. When packing for the return trip, you can simply toss the unused amounts. Use a permanent marker on the film caps to identify the contents.

■ Fill your empty film canisters with laundry soap and use the cap to seal and prevent it from spilling. Toss when empty.

■ Use clear film canisters to keep change together when traveling to many different countries on a single trip.

■ Empty film canisters also make perfect containers for safety pins, sewing kits, and numerous other items.

■ Number your film containers as you take pictures and make a list of what each roll contains. Place your exposed film back in the original container. This will make recording your trip much easier once you're home.

More great travel tips

■ Secure the shoulder strap of your carry-on around your foot or chair leg when seated. This acts as an anchor if the bag is grabbed.

■ Copy jokes, riddles, songs, recipes, etc. on recipe cards to share with new friends and children along the way. If you have a special cake recipe and facilities are available, you can make one to share with foreigners.

■ When looking for local activities in a foreign city, check out the daily newspaper. The TV guide section can be understood in almost any language.

■ While traveling long distances, mail home paper "extras" and items accumulated along the way but don't want to throw out: city maps, tourist pamphlets, attraction stubs, and receipts for tax purposes. Pack a manila envelope in your luggage and keep these items inside until you're ready to mail it home.

■ If you're constantly traveling to the same destination, leave some duplicate toiletries there so you don't have to keep carrying them.

■ Along the same idea, leave an old sweater, winter coat and winter shoes (or summer items) so you don't have to pack so much every trip.

31 Reasons to Travel with a Bandana

Almost every household has one...a Bandana. The funny thing is, many people haven't thought of traveling with one. Available in almost every color and design imaginable they are one item that should be on every traveler's checklist. **They take up almost no room and are particularly helpful in hot climates.**

Here are some ideas on how to use a Bandana in your travels:

■ Luggage Identification

■ An emergency diaper

■ Keep your head warm

■ Ear warmer

■ Protect bald heads from sun

■ Protect the neck from the sun

■ Scarf or head covering for places of worship

■ Sweatband

■ Wear around neck damp to stay cool

■ Napkin

- Washcloth

- Travel Towel

- Rope

- First Aid- sling or bandage

- Knapsack

- Gift

- Bicycling (wrap around pant legs)

- Rag

- Face covering for dust/sun/cold

- To sit on in the woods or park bench

- Sink stopper

- Wave as a distress signal

- Put under your feet on a train seat

- Table cloth for picnics, trains, buses

- Ribbon to tie your hair back

- Cover pillow on the plane

- Handle on a bag

- A filter for water or coffee

- Tie 3 together = Belt or a top

- Handkerchief (the original use)

- To wave goodbye

And, one of my favorite, great ideas:

Travel journals are a wonderful way to keep memories along your journey, however they can be heavy to pack & can seem like a homework assignment at the end of a long day of sightseeing.

Well, for years my mother continually gave me travel journals as gifts and reminded me to jot down my travel experiences of all the exciting places I was going and all my adventures. Unfortunately, I was always too busy having fun to stop and "journal" but I did keep in touch with my family by sending postcards from around the world.

Guess what? My mother knew I wasn't writing in my journals and she collected every postcard & letter that I sent over the years and gave them back to me in boxes! I now have all those fantastic memories as keepsakes. (Mothers are so smart!).

Here's what I do today

As I travel, I purchase inexpensive postcards of my favorite sites, historical & cultural & even hotels, most of which have their own postcards. I pop a few postcards in my day bag & write them while I'm having lunch in a café or riding a train through the countryside. I jot down a special memory of the day, a favorite restaurant and its' location, anything.

Then I purchase the most interesting stamp I can find and mail the postcard…to myself!

The best part is I receive mail when I get home. It's fun to see how long it takes to receive them from different parts of the world and once received, here's what I do:

I punch a hole through the upper left hand corner and tie a ribbon around all the cards from my trip and place them on my coffee table. Not only is it a good conversational piece, but it keeps all the cards together. After a time, I place the neatly organized postcards into a shoe box (that I've decorated with maps) and catalog by trip. This way it's an easy reference for not only me, but when a friend asks, "What was the name of that great restaurant you raved about in Florence?" I can quickly locate it.

Tip: The people who take the postcard pictures are professionals and have the time to wait for the perfect weather, light, season etc.

so unless you're a professional photographer, you'll get a much better picture than with your own camera, and cheaper too.

More Great Post Card Tips

■ Visit a souvenir shop upon arrival in a city and look at the racks of postcards. This will give you a quick visual of many of the famous sights and areas in the city and give you some ideas of what interesting angles to photograph them.

■ When you develop your film ask for doubles and use them for postcards. Draw a line down the center of the back & put a note on one side & address on the other. Check w/post office if you're unsure of what is oversized & requires additional postage.

■ Collect postcards on your travels and use them to decorate your scrapbook or to make a collage under glass on your dresser. Display family postcards in shadow boxes.

■ Photo-mounting sleeves allow you to preserve your postcards in your scrapbook and are available at most craft stores. The sleeves allow you to easily slip the postcard in and out so you can enjoy both sides.

■ Another option for displaying your postcards in your scrapbook is to cut a window in your scrapbook page making both sides of the postcard visible.

■ Antique postcards are another fun item to collect and can be found in most cities worldwide.

■ Post cards usually contain some historical information on the back, which helps to organize your scrap book.

-16-
Family Travel Tips

There's no doubt that family travel makes memories…however what type of memories are made can depend on how prepared you are before you leave home.

Remember when planning family travel to take the age of each person into consideration. Each age has varying needs and varying needs means more to pack. Since more to pack translates into "what bags am I going to take?" and "how's it all going to fit?" here are some ideas on what bags to take and how to make the most of them. To make planning your trip easier there's also a checklist of what to pack in them.

Duffel bags are the perfect solution to packing large items usually needed by families, like strollers & car seats. Recently introduced are duffel bags with wheels. Consider these rolling duffels, which can be lifesavers when your bag is really loaded. They also make it easier for the kids to help out.

Small backpacks are great for children to carry on the plane or use in the car. Help each child/teenager pack their bag and include things to keep them busy like games, CD's w/headphones & snacks. Wrap up some small gifts to give them along the way, things you'd normally buy for the trip but it gives the added element of surprise.

A wheeled carry-on tote bag, which fits under the seat of the plane, is great for mom, dad or mature traveler who'd rather not carry their bag and is easily accessible when items are needed in flight.

And, plastic compression bags are the perfect solution to packing bulky items such as diapers, blankets & fleece jackets that can take up lots of room in your bag. Just squeeze out the air and you've saved up to 30% of valuable space. Great for stuffed animals.

Don't forget the space inside of shoes — it's amazing how much will fit inside of a teenager's shoe! Since the small shampoo, conditioner and cream bottles aren't enough for a week for a whole family, pack a full size bottle of shampoo, conditioner, cream rinse, etc. in a large resealable bag & stick it in their shoes. You can also stuff socks & underwear in there too!

By planning ahead, you'll save time & money and be able to enjoy valuable time with your family, instead of shopping for sunscreen when you'd rather be at the beach.

And remember this tip: Count your bags and family members as often as possible. You don't want to misplace either along the way.

Tips

- A great idea for packing children's clothing is to put an entire days outfit (including underwear and socks) in a large freezer bag and write the child's name on the outside of the bag. This helps when traveling with more than one child and saves time searching through luggage for individual items.

- Don't forget the need to pack play clothes if traveling on a more formal trip. Children will always find time to get dirty.

- A bandana is good for an emergency diaper!

- When traveling with children, get them involved. From the first moment you start planning your trip up to and including the packing. Start with hanging a map on the wall (at their eye-level) and highlight the route you'll be taking.

- Purchase used toys at garage sales to keep kids entertained without spending a lot of money.

- Wrap small surprise travel essentials that you'd give your children anyway and make them into gifts that you can hand out through out a long travel day. Disposable camera, etc. Be sure not to wrap anything you're taking on a plane.

- Have them decide a week in advance what clothes to take & after they're washed, put them aside so their clean for the trip.

■ Pack disposable diapers in an extra suitcase & you'll have an additional bag to use for purchases on your way home!

■ Pack a few extra nylon duffel and tote bags that you can use for beach bags, picnics, etc. along the way.

■ Use colored tote bags for different family members.

■ Coordinate colored nylon duffels for specific tasks, like "red" for dirty laundry and "green" for clean.

■ Here's a fun project: Have your children help you make bag tags for each of the bags. Neon colored construction paper and bright pens & stickers will keep them busy for hours. Cover with clear contact paper to help protect them and punch a hole & thread a brightly colored shoelace to tie it on the bag/backpack. For safety never put your child's name on the tag, just fun designs. They'll have a blast spotting their bag in a crowded baggage terminal.

■ When traveling with your children, keep a recent photo of your children with you at all times in case you become separated from them.

Beach Tips

■ Pack an inflatable kids swimming pool for a trip to the beach. Tides can be dangerous for children & the water really cold, so fill it up and keep it away from the water (always with an adult in attendance). Kids can still make sand castles and stay cool with water from the pool. And the water gets warm quickly from the solar heat.

■ Keep an inexpensive waterproof camera in your beach bag to catch some great shots in and out of the water. Keep your good camera away from the sand & salt water.

■ Don't forget biodegradable travel soap to rinse out salt water from expensive swim suits. It also works on your body and as shampoo.

■ Flip flops (thongs) are your friends and are a must for scary
  public showers, hot sandy beaches and hot concrete parking lots.

■ To travel lighter, pack a double duty sunscreen & insect
  repellent in one spray!

■ Don't forget a lightweight, long sleeve shirt and a pair of long
  pants. These can protect against wind and/or save your skin if
  you find you've had too much sun

Family Travel Checklist

Here is a list of items to consider taking with you, depending on
the age of the traveler. Some are a must; others are optional,
depending on your destination. Keep this list with each family
members clothing list to help organize your next trip.

Travel Bags

❏ Wheeled duffel bag(s)

❏ Small backpack for each child

❏ Backpack for each adult

❏ Wheeled carry-on tote

❏ Extra collapsible tote bag(s)

Family Essentials

❏ Diapers

❏ Car Seats (check each state's requirements)

❏ Window sunscreen

❏ Sunscreen/hat

❏ Umbrella Stroller

❏ Convertible stroller/backpack

❏ Collapsible crib

❏ Blanket/pillow

❏ Pacifier

❏ Ear plugs

❏ Cell Phone/charger

❏ Walkie-talkies (or 2 cell phones)

❏ First aid kit

❏ Medications

❏ Night Light

❏ Electrical outlet covers

❏ Antibacterial Hand Sanitizer

❏ Easy-care, easy-wear clothing

Food

❏ Water Bottles w/water not juice

❏ Healthy snacks (not greasy chips)

❏ Picnic supplies

❏ Tippy cups, plastic bowls

❏ Pre-moistened towelettes

Children's Basic Weekend Travel Wardrobe

❏ 2-3 T-Shirts

❏ 1-2 pair Shorts

❏ 1-2 pair pants

❏ 3-4 underpants

❏ 2-3 Socks

❏ Sneakers

❑ Sandals or thongs

❑ Swimsuit and beach towel

❑ Sunglasses

❑ Pajamas

❑ Long sleeved shirt

❑ Sweatshirt/sweatpants

❑ Rain jacket with hood

❑ Hat, gloves, boots

❑ Dress clothes/shoes/coat (if appropriate)

Toys

❑ CD player/headphones/batteries

❑ Inflatable Beach ball

❑ Colored pencils (Crayons can melt)

❑ Bubbles (fun at any age)

❑ New toy

-17-
Travel Gift Ideas

Whether you are traveling to visit old friends, or just making new friends along the way, it is always a nice gesture to bring a gift. It doesn't need to be an expensive gift, and obviously, the easier it is to pack the better. It's the thought that counts.

Keep in mind when you are selecting presents that anything with a place name or logo on it is treasured by foreigners. In addition, something with a picture of your home state or region is very interesting to others and leads to engaging conversation.

And instead of using valuable space in your luggage packing wrapping paper & ribbons, pack a few small gift bags. Throw in a few gift cards & you're ready to celebrate any special occasion on the road.

The following are some gift ideas that are easy to pack & lightweight:

Balloons Unbreakable and fun to play with, hold them behind your back and have children guess what color the balloon is, and the first one who guesses correctly wins the balloon. If you do this, for example in Spanish, you then teach them the color in English. It can be done anywhere in the world in any language.

Bubbles Anywhere you go in the world, children love bubbles. They produce instant smiles! Pack inside lots of plastic bags.

Playing Cards With fun pictures on them. National Parks, Flags, your company logo, Cartoon Characters, anything that's unique.

Specialty Foods Small pre-packaged treats such as premium nuts, chocolate truffles, etc., make great gifts (as long as they will travel well).

Digital Camera A fun way to immediately share some photos & entertain new friends along the way.

Polaroid Camera Take a Polaroid camera for instant pictures. It's also a great icebreaker with new friends.

Frisbee A Frisbee packs easily and is lots of fun, especially with printing on it from a sporting event or large city. This also may begin a game or two along the route and is great exercise as well.

Picture Calendar A calendar from your home region is a greatly appreciated gift and a useful one. It packs flat on the bottom of your suitcase and allows you to share the beautiful areas near your home, which may be very different from the country you're in. They'll remember you every month.

Pins Any type of pins are fun and can be worn on almost anything; hats, lapels, sweaters, anywhere. From your local regatta to the state flower.

Pens/Pencils Are a popular gift idea. A variety of colors and sizes is appreciated by all ages. They make good tips and gifts for people along the way, as some customs do not allow monetary gratuities.

Baseball Hats/Scarf Light weight and easy to pack, these are easy items to take with you. A hat with the logo of your favorite team or sport is great.

Stickers From elections, sporting events, or your own home town, stickers are fun for children as well as adults.

Holiday Ornaments For a memorable gift or souvenir, ornaments don't take up much space in your luggage. Every year when you unpack your ornaments it's like taking a trip around the world. From Nutcrackers discovered in Germany to boomerangs from Australia, ornaments make unique and special gifts.

And…before you leave home, make up a gift list of everyone you intend to remember with a gift upon your return. Start with the most important and continue down. Don't forget the cat sitter or the neighbor who takes care of your home while you are gone.

Plan in advance & pack bubble wrap if you're packing something breakable. If you're looking for a special poster or piece of art, poster tubes can really be difficult to find when traveling. Pack one in your suitcase and use the inside of the tube to pack your socks and other squishible — non wrinkling items — clothing.

And…don't forget all the great travel essentials that are mentioned throughout this book make wonderful useful gifts through out the year for family & friends at home and along your travels. A hanging toiletry kit is a wonderful graduation gift for a student going off to college and new luggage is a generous and much appreciated wedding gift.

"Don't forget to take half the clothes and twice the money you think you'll need."

Author Unknown

The Ultimate
Travelers Checklist

Here it is! A quick reference checklist to help get you organized before you pack your bags. This is a list of items to consider taking with you, depending on your destination. Some are a must, others are optional. Keep this list with your own personal clothing list to help organize your next trip. Please refer to pages 135-136 for children's items. Also included are some essential tips to prepare you & your home for your trip.

Find some time a few weeks before your trip & go through the list, checking off items that you think you might need. This will give you time to get items that you need for your trip without last minute shopping. Feel free to make copies for ease of use — or print them from my website at www.packitup.com.

This checklist (beginning on the next page) probably includes the entire contents of your house. Check only items that you think will be essential for each destination. Be sure to make copies in order to have extras ready for your next trip!

Happy Travels from Pack It Up!
www.packitup.com

The Ultimate Traveler's Checklist

Home Checklist

❏ Stop Deliveries

❏ Have Post Office hold mail

❏ Arrange for care of pets, lawn and houseplants

❏ Set-up a timed night lighting system

❏ Notify local police of your absence

❏ Leave house key & trip itinerary with a neighbor, plus contact information and insurance numbers.

❏ Empty refrigerator

❏ Eliminate possible fire hazards (unplug appliances, etc.)

❏ Turn down thermostat

❏ Turn off water heater

❏ Reconfirm with airlines

❏ Store valuables in a safe place

❏ Lock all doors and windows

Pre-Departure

❏ Passport & Visas

❏ Health Documentation

❏ Transportation Tickets

❏ Student ID/Hostel Pass

❏ Emergency Information

❏ International Drivers License

❏ Insurance

❏ Hotel Reservations

❏ Traveler's Checks

❏ Small amount of local Currency

❏ Credit Cards/ATM Card

❏ Trip Cancellation Insurance

❏ Medical Insurance

❏ Personal Identification

❏ Extra Passport Photos

❏ Only keys needed upon return home

❏ Photocopies of all Documentation

Safety & Security

❏ Security Wallet

❏ Passport Cover

❏ ID/Boarding Pass Holder

❏ Neon ID Tags

❏ Neon Luggage Tags & Straps

❏ Neon Cable Ties

❏ Adjustable-length Cable Lock

Safety & Security *(con't)*

- ❏ Combination Locks
- ❏ Cell Phone & Adapter
- ❏ Rubber Door Stopper
- ❏ Travel Smoke Alarm
- ❏ Whistle/Compass Combo

Basics

- ❏ Luggage
- ❏ Convertible Day Bag
- ❏ Small Day Pack
- ❏ Travel Clothing
- ❏ Rain Coat with Hood
- ❏ Gloves, Hat (visor or brimmed)
- ❏ Camera, Film
- ❏ Camera Batteries
- ❏ Video Camera, Tapes
- ❏ Laptop Computer
- ❏ Computer Equipment
- ❏ Water Bottle
- ❏ Healthy Snack
- ❏ Language Books
- ❏ Travel Watch/Alarm
- ❏ Guidebooks/Maps
- ❏ Highlighter Pen/Marker
- ❏ Reading Material
- ❏ Notepad/Pens/Pencils

- ❏ Address Book/Labels
- ❏ Postcards/Family Photos
- ❏ Travel Alarm Clock
- ❏ Swimsuit
- ❏ Bandana/Scarf/Pareo
- ❏ Games/Playing Cards
- ❏ Binoculars
- ❏ Pocket Knife
- ❏ Flashlight
- ❏ Anti-bacterial Hand Sanitizer

Personal Care Items

- ❏ Hanging Toiletry Kit
- ❏ Comb/Brush
- ❏ Toothbrush/Paste
- ❏ Toothbrush Cap Covers
- ❏ Shampoo/Conditioner
- ❏ Sunscreen/Lip Balm
- ❏ Dental Floss
- ❏ Tissues/Toilet Paper
- ❏ Toilet Seat Covers
- ❏ Mouthwash
- ❏ Deodorant
- ❏ Feminine Hygiene Products
- ❏ Soap-Personal
- ❏ Skin Care Moisturizer
- ❏ Skin Care Toner & Cleanser

Personal Care Items *(con't)*

- ❏ Body Lotion/Body Powder
- ❏ Cotton Balls/Q-tips
- ❏ Shatterproof Mirror
- ❏ Make Up/Remover Pads
- ❏ Nail Polish/Remover Pads
- ❏ Nail File/Nail Clippers
- ❏ Tweezers
- ❏ Travel Perfume Atomizer
- ❏ Slippers/Socks
- ❏ Travel Bubble Bath
- ❏ Razor & Shaving Cream
- ❏ Travel Towel/Washcloth
- ❏ Shower Cap/Thongs
- ❏ Plastic Travel Bottles
- ❏ Retractable Razor
- ❏ Dual Voltage Hairdryer
- ❏ Dual Voltage Curling Iron
- ❏ Extra Eye Glasses/Repair Kit
- ❏ Contacts/Contact Lens
- ❏ Cleaner/Solution

Medical

Always consult your personal physician or local health center for help in planning your trip medication needs.

- ❏ Prescription Medication
- ❏ Insulated Bag for Medication (if needed)

- ❏ First Aid Kit
- ❏ Aspirin/Pain Reliever
- ❏ Collapsible Cup
- ❏ Antihistamines
- ❏ Thermometer
- ❏ Cold Medicine
- ❏ Diarrhea Medicine
- ❏ Pepto-Bismol®/ Alka-Seltzer®
- ❏ Laxative
- ❏ Insect Repellent
- ❏ Dental Repair Kit
- ❏ Sunscreen
- ❏ Lip Balm
- ❏ Sunburn Relief
- ❏ Antibiotic Cream
- ❏ Moleskin
- ❏ Motion Sickness/Jet Lag Remedy
- ❏ Personal Hygiene Items
- ❏ Water Purification System
- ❏ Vitamins

Comfort Items

- ❏ Neck Pillow, Eye Shades, Ear Plugs
- ❏ Travel Blanket
- ❏ Inflatable Lumbar Pillow
- ❏ Eye drops

Comfort Items *(con't)*
- ❏ Removable Shoe Inserts
- ❏ CD Player/CD's
- ❏ Book on Cassette
- ❏ Photos From Home
- ❏ Travel Journal/Postcards
- ❏ Flask

Laundry on the Go
- ❏ Multi-Purpose Travel Soap
- ❏ Micro-fiber Travel Towel
- ❏ Braided Elastic Laundry Line
- ❏ Inflatable Hangers
- ❏ Sink Stopper
- ❏ Stain Stick Remover
- ❏ Clothes Pins
- ❏ Sewing Kit
- ❏ Mesh Bag for Dirty Laundry
- ❏ Dryer Sheets
- ❏ Travel Iron
- ❏ Travel Steamer
- ❏ Lint Brush

Packing Essentials
- ❏ Compression Bags
- ❏ Packing Folders
- ❏ Packing Cubes
- ❏ Resealable Plastic Bags
- ❏ Additional Expandable Tote

Additional Items
- ❏ Money Exchanger/ Calculator
- ❏ Coin Organizer
- ❏ Duct Tape/String
- ❏ Travel Umbrella
- ❏ Disposable Waterproof Camera
- ❏ Dice
- ❏ Calculator
- ❏ Scissor
- ❏ Waterproof Neck Pouch
- ❏ Collapsible Cup
- ❏ Powdered Energy Drink
- ❏ Small Tape Recorder
- ❏ Stationary
- ❏ Expandable Tote Bag
- ❏ Extension cord
- ❏ Pareo
- ❏ Flip Flops
- ❏ Evening Bag
- ❏ Travel Jewelry Case
- ❏ Travel Umbrella
- ❏ Corkscrew/Bottle Opener/ Straw
- ❏ Picnic Supplies
- ❏ Hot Pot
- ❏ Voltage Converters/ Adapters
- ❏ Collapsible Cane

Additional Items *(con't)*

- ❏ Book Light
- ❏ Rubber Bands/Paper Clips
- ❏ Business Cards
- ❏ Tape Measure
- ❏ Bubble Plastic (breakables)
- ❏ Extra Shoelaces
- ❏ Sunglasses/Sunscreen/Hat
- ❏ Walkie Talkies
- ❏ Backseat Organizer
- ❏ Sleepsack (silk/cotton)
- ❏ Short Wave Radio
- ❏ Insect Repellent
- ❏ Emergency Blanket
- ❏ Rain Poncho
- ❏ Mosquito Netting
- ❏ A Positive Attitude

Easy Gifts to Pack

- ❏ Playing Cards
- ❏ Bubbles
- ❏ Frisbee
- ❏ Bandanna/Hat/Scarf
- ❏ Inflatable Beach Ball

"Always pack your respect for
people of different cultures."

Anne McAlpin

Resources

Transportation Security Administration
www.tsa.gov

Federal Aviation Administration
www.faa.gov

Travel Goods Association
www.travel-goods.org

American Society of Travel Agents
www.astanet.com

CLIA- Cruise Lines International Assoc.
www.cruising.org

Medic Alert Foundation
(888) 633-4298
www.medicalert.com

World Health Organization
www.who.int

U.S. Department of State
www.state.gov

US State Department Travel Advisories and Consular Fact Sheets
http://travel.state.gov/travel_warnings.html

CIA World Fact Book
www.cia.gov/cia/publications/factbook/index.html

Zierer Visa Services
www.zvs.com

To The Traveler

Travel Tip Contest

If in your travels you discover a new packing or travel tip that is not already included in Pack It Up, please enter it in our Travel Tip Contest at **www.packitup.com**.

All Travel Tip Winners will receive a Pack It Up Travel Essentials Gift Bag filled with items no traveler should leave home without!

Contact Anne

You can reach Anne directly at **anne@packitup.com**.

Happy Travels!

Pack It Up Seminars

To find out more about Pack It Up
Traveling Smart & Safe Seminars,
please go to www.packitup.com.

A woman once told me

that before anyone in her family takes a trip,

she lends them her Pack It Up book.

When they return, she asks that

they write in the back of the book

a little bit about their trip:

Their destination, their favorite tip

from the book and their favorite new tip

they learned along the way.

Her book has become a treasured

family journal.

Notes & Quotes

"People don't take trips — trips take people."

John Steinbeck

Notes & Quotes

"The only way to be sure of catching a train is to miss the one before it."

G.K. Chesterton (1874-1936)

Notes & Quotes

_____

_____

_____

_____

_____

_____

_____

_____

_____

_____

_____

_____

_____

_____

*"The shortest distance between two points
is usually under repair."*

Unknown

Notes & Quotes

_____

_____

_____

_____

_____

_____

_____

_____

_____

_____

_____

_____

"I never travel without my diary.

One should always have something

sensational to read in the train."

Oscar Wilde (1856-1900)

Notes & Quotes

_____

_____

_____

_____

_____

_____

_____

_____

_____

_____

_____

_____

_____

*"The world is a book, and those who
do not travel read only a page."*

St. Augustine (354-430)

Notes & Quotes

"He who hesitates is not only lost,
but miles from the next exit."

Unknown

"Always pack your sense of humor."

Anne McAlpin